THE EPISCOTAPE
LETTERS

THE EPISCOTAPE
LETTERS

A series of satirical essays on the state of The Episcopal Church
and their implications for the wider Anglican Communion

David W. Virtue

J2B PUBLISHING

J2B Publishing LLC
4251 Columbia Park Road
Pomfret, MD 20675
www.J2BLLC.com

This book is set in Garamond

Cover image by Minerva Studio/Shutterstock.com
ID: 670263205

ISBN: 978-1-948747-53-0

DEDICATION

This book is dedicated to Malcolm Muggeridge one of the most brilliant and controversial figures of the twentieth century who took me under his wing when I was a student in London in the Sixties. He once described himself as "vendor of words". His creative and superb use of the English language made him one of the greatest journalists of his time, perhaps the greatest. His mentoring skills gave me the impetus and stimulus to be a Christian journalist. I will always be in his debt.

David W. Virtue, DD

FOREWORD

The Screwtape Letters written by the late C.S. Lewis has become a model for satire about the current state of the Anglican Communion, especially the Episcopal Church.

In my own more modest attempts I have attempted to emulate the great Lewis with my own reflections on the state of The Episcopal Church through this literary device. I began writing them in 2004 and I continue to write them to this present day.

I have chosen the names Teufel and Faust as the senior and junior devil in these letters. Teufel is a devil, a creature of hell, a demon, a fallen angel from German mythology. Faust is a charlatan who makes a pact with the Devil, exchanging his soul for unlimited knowledge and worldly pleasures.

I have also added a number of miscellaneous essays at the conclusion of these Episcotape letters for your reading enjoyment.

More of my writings on the Anglican Communion can be read here: www.virtueonline.org
and on Facebook: https://facebook.com/virtueonline/

ACKNOWLEDGMENTS

The increasing implosion of the Episcopal Church with its headlong departure from the "faith once delivered" in order to accommodate itself to a secular culture is a heartbreaking experience for one who has loved and served in his Church (in some official capacity since childhood) for some 77 years.

The church's leadership in its doctrinal blindness explains the staggering loss of half of its membership on demographic lines - that the loss of membership is due to society being secular and not a time to be supporting churches.

Such pathology cries out for correction and there is no better way to do so than by humor and satire. There are few as knowledgeable and talented to do so as David Virtue. Using C. S. Lewis' Screwtape Letters as a model he exposes in accurate and telling ways the foibles and self-destruct machinations of the Episcopal Church's apostasy.

David Virtue has over the years been a tenacious witness and an incomparably courageous reporter. We owe him profound gratitude and thank God for him.

- The Rt. Rev. Dr. C. FitzSimons Allison (SC ret.)

I have known David for fifty years to be a courageous and perceptive Christian journalist whose work has informed the Anglican world of the painful realities of the inroads of the secular culture into the institutional church. His clever satirical writing chronicles the decline of biblical orthodoxy in the Episcopal Church, the surrender to the zeitgeist, the persecution of the faithful clergy, the apostasy and vindictiveness of the hierarchy and the birth of new Anglican congregations and jurisdictions. His contributions will serve as an important historical source and contemporary witness in the future.

- The Rev. Ted Schroder, author, pastor and blogger at www.tedschroder.com.

TABLE OF CONTENTS

THE EPISCOTAPE LETTERS

SEXUAL FREEDOM

My Dear Teufel,

News of your enormous success with American mainline Protestant denominations has reached us down here. We view with great glee your ability to undermine "the faith once delivered" to these gullible Americans.

Their cries for "freedom" and autonomy of thought have nicely backfired in our favor. Having people think independently of each other without an over-riding theology holding them all together has been one of your great successes. Keep it up.

It would appear that your greatest success though has been in the area of sexuality. As you know, we didn't invent that, the Other Side did. We, and particularly yourself, have been very effective in undermining and distorting it in our favor.

You have been particularly successful in doing this with all generations of Americans, not just the young. Internet pornography has been marvelously helpful. Pedophilia is undermining the Catholic Church to our advantage. Americans don't like to be tied down (if you'll pardon the pun) to one view of sexual behavior and this has worked marvelously in our favor.

Take that disgusting institution called marriage. It has been a disaster up to this point to keep people monogamous and faithful to the same partner for years and years. We have tried endlessly to undermine it with very little success. Until recently. Then, my dear Teufel, you managed to get a group of very bright (bright is always best) intellectual sodomites to come up with the idea of committed same-sex relationships with marriage rites to boot. This is nothing short of brilliant and our Father will honor you with his special award next time you are down here.

This is a brilliant master plan that seems to be working most effectively in the churches which have taken the lead with society following behind and politicians falling all over themselves to endorse sodomite acceptance. This has been a most effective strategy.

It would seem, by your letters to us, that the American Episcopal Church has been in the vanguard of this movement. Absolutely brilliant.

You have taken the country's premier denomination, which has seen more than eleven presidents, countless self-serving politicians, and an endless supply of intellectuals, historians and theologians, and bundled them into believing a worldview that endorses a behavior that actually kills people.

And they do this in the name of "justice" and "peace" dismissing any talk of morality as arcane and "fundamentalist." We especially like the term "no common mind". It is a breeding ground for moderate men of all shades of opinion to express themselves and to feel particularly self-righteous when they can't agree, but they all drink champagne together, anyway.

We, The Supreme Council of Hades, salute you in your endeavors. You have cleverly moved the whole discussion away from morality and holiness to one of "body parts" as the Episcopal Bishop of Massachusetts put it and "what happens below the waistline is really none of anybody's business." Of course it isn't. The lie must continue.

The freedom to have sexual relations with whomever must be forefront and center in your campaign to undermine traditional mores. The more you do this, the more sexual chaos reigns. That works definitely in our favor.

You will have noticed, I'm sure, that once people move away from acceptable -- read biblical moral standards (how I hate that term) -- they are easily seduced in more fundamental ways about how life should be lived and what people OUGHT to believe about God and His word (though we are doing our best to undermine that).

That incredible find in Bishop John Shelby Spong has been music to our ears. His Twelve Theses effectively dismissed the entire corpus of Christian Faith. I can assure you and him, that when he arrives here, as surely he will since he is well over 80, that a special place of darkness is reserved for him.

Be careful how you use him. He is too obviously heretical which could backfire. The cowardly American Episcopal House of Bishops has never had the guts to put him on trial and toss him out for his utterances. That, too, has worked in our favor. At another level he is too obviously apostate which could provide the basis for a backlash.

Work on the moderate bishops, they're your best hope and ours. They gave up the faith a long time ago (most of them can't say the creed without crossing their fingers,) but they couch their unbelief in terms far more acceptable to their Episcopal flocks. Undermine the faithful a little piece at a time. Chip away at the faith bit-by-bit, and doctrine-by-doctrine. Start with the Nicene Creed. When it is all over they won't know what they believe. They will all end up in hell with us.

Keep them using phrases like "diversity" and "pluriformity" and toss in the word "fundamentalist" - a grand and glorious word - when things look like we might be losing a few to the other side.

For hell's sake, keep talking up good works. Those Millennium Development Goals are, if you'll pardon the lapse of good taste, heaven sent. Their recent past Presiding Bishop Katharine Jefferts Schori floated around the world talking about how the whole world could be saved if invoked long enough and loud enough. That she kept away from talking about souls that needed saving, an afterlife of heaven... of being with HIM if they repent of their sins, was a stroke of genius. That she refrained from discussing anything supernatural, of focusing on eternal life through the cross and keeping it this worldly, was masterful.

I must say your work in getting those Episcopal seminaries to drop from their curricula anything about the Atonement was nothing short of brilliant. All that talk of the cross being "child abuse" by bishops like Spong, is music to our ears.

Keep bludgeoning the bible as an outdated, unreliable source for people. If they must read it, tell them it is quaint history with some fanciful ideas concerning miracles and myths about virgin births. Move the whole discussion into the area of fantasy following Harry Potter. Much better to discredit it by poking holes and fun at it than blindly burning bibles. That never works.

It looks like your real work lies with those Episcopalians. The primates of the Anglican Communion have set a deadline wherein the Episcopal Church must make up its mind about a number of issues including ordaining sodomites to the priesthood and performing same-sex marriages.
If they stick to this deadline it will be a disaster for us. It will split the whole Anglican Communion into good guys and bad guys. Then we will have to go work on the good guys again.

Whatever you do, keep them all at the table. Fudge and blur the lines. The Hegelian Archbishop, Rowan Williams, who is really firmly on our side, must keep the language loose. The American House of Bishops must manipulate him when he visits there. Make sure the Episcopal Church is given a clean bill of spiritual health and keep pushing the Covenant as a way forward. Push hermeneutics as another step forward in prevarication. Under no circumstances is the Episcopal Church to get thrown out of the communion. I have another junior devil working on the Global South Primates.

Fudge and weave and get them to resurrect a report presented to the Primates' Meeting prepared by a small group within the Joint Primates-ACC Standing Committee that said the Episcopal Church had met two of the three requests of the Windsor Report and deserves a reprieve.

Above all keep the party going and keep them all together. If the Bishop of Pittsburgh Robert Duncan gets too far out of line, isolate him and the Network bishops and make them look like nasty uninclusive schismatics. If you'll pardon the pun, beat the hell into them for their lack of inclusivity and diversity and their constant harping on about absolute truth, which is really the kiss of death to us.

I firmly believe, my dear Wormhole, that we can actually undermine the whole Anglican Communion, given time, and we have plenty of that. Under no circumstances must you allow them to split into two parties - one big communion of fudge is more to our liking, in that way we can eventually undermine the whole thing and bring it all over to our side.

I remain your affectionate uncle,

Faust

EPISCOPAL BISHOPS MEET IN NEW ORLEANS

My dear Teufel,

Events are unfolding perfectly in our favor, but don't count your chickens. Things are far from a done deal. Our Enemy has a trick or two up his sleeve that could derail everything.

We have been close, many times in history to outright victory, only to have it snatched from us at the last moment. Be very careful how you go.

The upcoming meeting of the American House of Bishops in New Orleans will be a defining moment that you must use wisely and carefully. New Orleans itself is a victim of Hurricane Katrina. There it will be ripe for Episcopal Church leaders to paint themselves as victims of fundamentalist Global South primates. They will tell Dr. Rowan Williams they are ecclesiastical victims. They will draw parallels to the Lower Ninth Ward and how America and President George Bush abandoned this place and its people. They will draw parallels about the way they are being treated by those horrible orthodox African types.

Williams will be made to feel their outrage of abandonment and pain. Doing so will remove some of the psychological harshness posed by the Dar es Salaam deadline.

This city was chosen for a particular reason and I suspect your hand was in it. You are to be congratulated. It is a wildly decadent city much like the Episcopal Church; their morals parallel one other. Make sure the handful of sodomite bishops is taken care of in the French Quarter and that the alcohol runs freely. The freer the alcohol flows, the faster the morals fly out the door.

Now it is very important, in private discussions between Presiding Bishop Jefferts Schori and Williams, that Williams is made aware of the fact that without TEC's money Lambeth won't happen and the Anglican Consultative Council will cease to exist in any meaningful way. Williams knows this of course, and he won't bite the hand that feeds him. But he MUST be reminded.

That horrible retired Bishop of Eau Claire fellow, William Wantland, recently told the Anglican Communion Network conference in Dallas that the Church of England will never forsake the Episcopal Church because it has money, which the Anglican Communion office desperately needs. This must not be said publicly, it must all be done privately, but the point must be made that without the millions needed to keep the whole show going, it would, in fact, collapse.
The fine art of manipulation must be brought into play. Work on this. The combination of "justice for homosexuals and lesbians" and "manipulation by money" must go hand in hand. Williams, as brilliant as he is, will be seduced. Remember he has already sent out the invitations

for Lambeth next year. To withdraw them now would be personally humiliating. See that he doesn't do it. A mild remonstrance from him to the HOB about the Episcopal Church's "timing", breaking the "bonds of affection" and not coming to a "common mind" is in order but nothing stronger. Make sure he talks up the Covenant as the great salvation paper that will rescue the Anglican Communion from itself.

Make sure Williams has a private meeting over coffee with sodomite Bishop Gene Robinson to remind him that he is in complete and total sympathy with the homogenital bishop, but that he can't say anything publicly to support him lest it upset the Global South Primates. Have the archbishop tell Robinson that the next time he comes to London to look him up at Lambeth Palace where he will arrange a private dinner with him and Jeffrey John, the gay Dean of St. Albans, his close personal friend.

Now make sure that when Williams talks to the HOB that he focuses on "spirituality." We love that word. The Council of Hades chortles every time we hear the word. One can make the word mean whatever one wants it to mean. The word has almost nothing to do with historic Christianity. We have raised a new generation of New Agers who talk endlessly about spirituality, which often goes along with nude Yoga, eating berries of indeterminate origin, coupled with a lot of gut grasping wheat germ. A lot of this "spirituality" talk has flowed over into the Episcopal Church with remarkable effectiveness in retreats given by those in sympathy with Hindu and Muslim spirituality as well as the "spirituality" of sodomy. Resurrect Rumi the Sufi. Spirituality is the new buzzword; play it up.

Also play up "prayer". That's another all-encompassing meaningless word. Oh, for the good ol' days when Presiding Bishop Frank Griswold was around. He often talked about prayer as "sending out good thoughts into the universe", especially after he survived prostate cancer. We were happy to oblige him. This might also be an occasion when Pennsylvania Bishop Charles Bennison's Visigoth Rite could be presented to the House of Bishops as another way, as he often says, "to move forward" with TEC's new religion.

While the Network bishops are lost to us, the Windsor bishops are still our best hope. They recently had a meeting in Texas and heard from Canon Geoffrey Cameron, William's hatchet man on the Anglican Consultative Council. He flew in to stiffen the spines of the Windsor bishops so they will not cave into a small minority of fundamentalists in the HOB. He is brilliant, shrewd and a personal friend of Rowan Williams. He speaks for him. He is, of course, totally in our corner and works brilliantly to keep the evanescent Canon Kenneth Kearon, his master, fully informed. Texas Bishop Don Wimberly, a real fence sitter, whose diocese is as rich as sin is secretly in our camp but likes to play up his "moderate" status. Make sure he does not fold.

It was Kearon, who you will recall, who flew to Canada and told their Synod that under no circumstances would the Canadian Church ever be thrown out of the Communion regardless of how they voted on sodomite ceremonies and the like. They and he remain friends of the Archbishop of Canterbury.

In New Orleans, the seduction of Williams must be made complete. We know where he stands on the issues especially sodomy. That horrible

SPREAD paper put out by that fellow Dr. John Rodgers was truly an expose of the worst order, but it is out there, and we suspect that is why Bishop Robert Duncan made a point of saying at the meeting of the Anglican Communion Network in Dallas that "what is needed is a completely new structure Lambeth is failing, Canterbury is failing, the Anglican Consultative Council is prejudiced in a Western way and the primates are sadly divided north and south. We'll leave and they can take the stuff with them to hell, because that is where they will take it. This is Good Friday and we have to face it."

That statement almost undid us, Teufel. Our father was on the verge of sending you a bottle of his special preserve "bishop's blood" from the Pike oak cellar when Duncan uttered those infamous words. He point blank refused to send it, it upset him so much.

Earlier in the month, Bishop Rodgers expressed similar sentiments in an interview with that vulgar VirtueOnline news service saying that he thought that a major division of the Anglican Communion was likely.

UNDER NO CIRCUMSTANCES ARE YOU TO LET THIS HAPPEN, WORMHOLE. You have no idea how heavy our father's grip will be on you if you fail in this mission. The Anglican Communion must hold together regardless of what happens. We can only win if they are all made to stay on the same page. Less than three years ago some 17 primates refused to take holy communion with Griswold; now it is down to single digit numbers in Tanzania earlier this year over Mrs. Jefferts Schori. We will whittle and wear them down, one primate at a time. And make sure that before all the bishops leave New Orleans that they do the Circle Dance of Dispossession. I must say that the video you sent down to us last time had us in total glee.

Mark my words, Wormhole, we have all the time in the world. In fact, we have the world and the darkness of the world has enveloped the Episcopal Church. All praise to our father in Hell.

Keep us posted on developments as they unfold. We shall be watching you closely.

I remain your affectionate uncle,

Faust

LESBIAN CANDIDATE FOR BISHOP OF CHICAGO

My dear Teufel,

The day fast approacheth, and the night is already here. It is night and darkness in The Episcopal Church. It is important that it stays that way. Beware the shaft of light that, by mistake, lightens the odd liberal bishop into the realization that he might be wrong. Especially keep an eye on Bishop Russell Jacobus of Fond du Lac. He shows signs of weakening. He once had that abominable faith, but under pressure, and that wonderful thing called collegiality, he folded like a pack of (HOB) cards. Lose him and you are burnt toast.

The Council of Hades was especially gleeful at the announcement this past week that a lesbian living in a committed relationship (we especially love that "committed" bit, tis music to our ears), is on the slate to be the next bishop of the Episcopal Diocese of Chicago. That great line of hers, "My partner, Emily Ingalls (a cradle Episcopalian), is the gift that most sustains me," had our father chortling. Little does she know what REALLY sustains her.

You must move all hell to see that she wins. We do not want a replay of the Diocese of Newark, where a sodomite got thrown out on the first ballot. Most humiliating. Make sure her nomination goes to the bitter end. Have Ms. Russell of Integrity fame send out repeated messages of whine and inclusion to all the HOB. They will help us enormously.

The timing of her nomination could not have been better - right in the middle of those dreadful consecrations in Africa which unnerved, albeit briefly, our father who is doing his best to undermine those African archbishops. He has sent agent Slubnose to work on that Bishop Mwamba fellow in Botswana. What a find he has turned out to be. Slubnose is working hard to see that he becomes the next Archbishop of Central Africa to replace Malango. If he does, Mwamba will bring in Henderson...the province will be ours.

Make sure Louie Crew and every pansexual you can incite plead Tracey Lind's cause before the bar of sodomite justice. She MUST win Chicago, Teufel. A victory here seals the deal. We will close the last loop of pansexual acceptance. It will be a rout of the highest order.

Nonetheless, our father and the Council remain concerned and somewhat fearful.

The polarizing effect of this event could cause things to backfire. In history, we have often overplayed our hand to the other side's success. Marginalizing those orthodox types can galvanize them into taking risks for their abominable master and kingdom. That is a real danger.

They will plead their cause to the Man from Nazareth, a cry that will not go unheard. Therein lies the problem. We do not know how He will come to their rescue, but He will; history has shown that. You must be on your guard.

Think back just a few years when we had most of Eastern Europe and the Soviet Union in our grip, but within 70 years, poof, it was gone. And one single man - Alexander Solzhenitsyn, undid it. Never underestimate the power of one, Teufel. NEVER! Those damned evangelicals have a way of turning things around.

The rise of materialism and Islam in Europe is indeed good news, but don't overplay your hand The rise of Christianity in China with the failure of Communism is a great blow to the Council. We had not anticipated it. The church grows daily by the tens of thousands. We thought the Chinese would replace Communism with a nascent, lifeless Buddhism, but that has not been the case.

Catholicism, which has grown stale in Latin America, has been challenged by Pentecostalism which is bringing new life into people with new churches. It is now a mighty force with millions of adherents to contend with. We are working hard to undermine it all, but it is not without much pain. We are THE masters of pain.

Pain causes doubt and doubt brings unbelief. Work on it. Work on fear, greed and power. Those Episcopalians and Anglicans truly love power. A purple shirt works much in our favor. It gives men feelings of superiority they have never had before. They can now throw their weight around and expect, and often get, obsequious subservience from the laity.

Use feelings of inadequacy, depression and the 'poor me's' to allow sexual indiscretion to have free reign among the clergy. Many orthodox pastors believe that God owes them. Make them believe it. Help them believe that God owes them a little sex on the side for all the good they do. In the end they are ours or at least neutered in their evangelistic efforts. Undermine and subvert, my dear Teufel. Undermine and subvert.

Work on egos. The bigger the ego, the bigger the downfall. We have seen it happen so many times. Hypocrisy is a wonderful weapon. Ted Haggard was a joy to work with. Humility is truly horrible, especially when we see it in people who can dominate with their words and smiles. Vile humility must be eradicated, Teufel. Press the need for power. The clenched fist and the raised phallus is sweet music to our ears.

When people start groveling before their god and confessing their sins, our father has apoplectic fits. We do love psychology. Making people feel good about themselves, building their self-esteem, "I can be me" -- whatever the hell that means -- eventually leads people into thinking they are bits of god, part of a godhead. People who go in search of themselves deserve exactly what they find. Tempt people into believing they really ARE god and can control their universes! It is the height of narcissistic arrogance. Keep people focused on themselves, their needs, and their desires. Under no circumstances must people be taught to rely on someone out there who really cares for them. Substitute god for a 'higher power' that does wonders for us. You know our father fears god and trembles, but that is not public knowledge. If people are taught to die and be reborn spiritually, we become powerless.

The final subversion of the Episcopal House of Bishops is at hand, Teufel. It will be a moment of triumph for our father and the council that has worked so hard to undermine it all. Forty years of steady erosion -- 'inchatatime' as Ms. Russell calls her blog. Now we come down to the last few yards. A final push is in order. Allow Mrs. Schori to hand the ball to Dr. Williams who will run it up the gut for a touchdown. It will be the final nail in the coffin for the Anglican Communion.

We are all watching you, Teufel. Our father embraces you.

I remain your affectionate uncle,

Faust

NEW ORLEANS VICTORY

My dear Teufel,

The Council of Hades and I have just learned the most excellent news! we salute your brilliant efforts in New Orleans!

Your efforts exceeded our wildest expectations and you know how high they were.

That you succeeded in turning the Hegelian mind of Rowan Williams to our advantage is nothing short of brilliant.

That you succeeded in making sure he stayed the course with Mrs. Jefferts Schori and the Episcopal House of Bishops, while, of course, listening to all sides of the arguments was a sterling performance.

Make sure the Law of Non-Contradiction never comes up on his radar screen, while the Law of Diminishing Returns only briefly pops into his mind as The Episcopal Church sinks slowly into the sunset.

Prevarication, obfuscation, muddling through (something the British are known for) should continue to be the order of the day. Keep them all "listening" (We do so love that word!) and participating in blessed "conversation", a pure Griswoldian. Under no circumstances must "conversation" end in resolution. It is absolutely forbidden. They must talk themselves to death, if necessary. Keep them talking till they keel over like ancient dinosaurs. When the last liberal bishop is talking to himself as the lights go out, make sure the waiter serves him a gin and tonic laced with cyanide. He should die nobly while talking to himself about Millennium Development Goals. Don't give a thought to Spong; he is firmly with us.

We were a little concerned that Rowan Williams may have overplayed his hand by saying that the new churches (Global South) should learn from the older churches (like his, the CofE and the American Episcopal Church). We understand that horrible Akinola fellow went ballistic when he heard this. What exactly did Rowan have in mind? Lectures on how to make churches grow? Litigate yourself into bankruptcy? Consecrating sodomites so millions of homosexuals will allegedly pour into Episcopal churches? We know it won't happen, but that is the sort of thing that unglues global south primates. For Hell's sake, keep him focused on everyone staying together at the table. Keep him preaching innocuous sermons about gratitude so they can all stay together at the communion table, and that "difference" is a sign, not of weakness, but of Anglican strength.

We do especially like all those lines about how different the Episcopal Church is from Southern Baptists because everything is grey and murky. It's the Via Media Church (not of course between Rome and non-conformity, but between sodomy and non sodomy) that will only be resolved if they wear down the other side. KEEP EVERYBODY

AT THE TABLE, Faust. Under no circumstances must anyone be allowed to leave.

We were mortified to hear that one of their number, a certain Bishop Jeffrey Steenson, hived off to Rome and told everyone right at the HOB meeting in New Orleans. This could have horrible consequences for everyone. It could lead to a minor revolt among the HOB. Herzog has gone. Now Steenson. Will Bob Duncan Bishop of Pittsburgh be far behind? He is very close to the Catholic bishops in Pittsburgh. We suspect he is doing more than just having coffee with the hierarchy. Does the word "conversation" come to mind? Kill such defections immediately and make sure they stay dead. Preach collegiality and community, another word we find most favorable in the pantheon of words to keep everyone at the table. The council noted, with great gravity, your sin of failure in this matter and you will be punished for it.

In the meantime keep the anger alive. The cries of outrage and the screams of Robinson at Williams about his "dehumanizing gays" go a long way to keeping the liberals galvanized. Make sure Robinson gets an observer invitation to Lambeth, but nothing more. Don't push the orthodox over the edge. A little guilt goes a long way. Play down talk of "ultimatums".

Now what truly troubles us is what took place recently in Pittsburgh. This is a disaster of the first order. Through the Sulphur we smell a new Anglican province aborning. This is a horrible thought to our Master. Those fractious Episcopalians will then have two churches, and we will have to go to work on the Righteous Ones. This is not good news, Teufel. It is much easier to undermine the orthodox if they stay than if they go. The Righteous Ones pay for the unrighteous goals of the liberals. If they and their money go, the liberals and revisionists will only lose. We cannot allow that. Persuade, cajole, but for hells sake keep them together. We will be watching you closely, Teufel.

I remain your affectionate uncle,

Faust

UNDERMINING THE FUNDAMENTALIST GLOBAL SOUTH

My dear Teufel,

The Council of Hades and I have been reviewing your latest missives and we have been most gleeful at your abilities to undermine those horrid, fundamentalist Primates in the Global South, especially that vile Archbishop Peter Akinola. That he has been joined by that Jensen fellow in Sydney and Venables in Argentina confirms our worst suspicions that schism is inevitable within the Anglican Communion.

This, however, is not necessarily to our liking. If there is a split, there will be identifiably good guys and bad guys, and we will have to go to work seriously on the good ones. By keeping them together, we can infiltrate and undermine the orthodox leaders. Look what you have achieved since Dromantine when 22 Primates refused to take Communion because Frank Griswold was present. That figure dropped to 8 in Dar es Salaam and it would drop even further if they stayed together. You must do everything in your power to keep them talking, Teufel, and at the same table.

We do love the way the word "conversation" is tossed about. It is sweet music to our ears. It was Griswold's mantra and has now become part of the avid vocabulary of Rowan Williams. Let them converse themselves to death, if need be, but keep them talking. By doing so, we can wear down those vile orthodox bishops and destroy them. The Windsor Report has failed so will the Covenant. Let them move on to hermeneutics to solve the problems in the communion. Sow in their minds that everyone can interpret Scripture from their own historical and cultural perspective, and therefore, there is no lasting or abiding or absolute truth about anything. This keeps the pansexual agenda alive and well, and we can use it to change the church's 2,000 track record on this.

Little do these fools know that fornication, adultery and homosexuality, if practiced, can destroy their souls. Hell is filled with such folk who believed they could do their own will. In doing so, they are really doing our will, the will of our father who is in Hades. Keep pressing the issue, undermine, undermine and undermine, again. Language is very important. Make sure the liberals keep talking about "fundamentalist" and "homophobic" bishops. Avoid words like Evangelical and Anglo-Catholic. Make sure that words like "inclusivity" and "justice", "patriarchy" and "rights" are lauded and used with great frequency. Keep words like "orientation" rather than "attraction" centered in the sex debate. It gives it the false air of genetic possibilities which we know is an illusion but they want to believe otherwise. It binds them closer to us Teufel and we wait in time to embrace them more fully.

I must tell you that getting that British evangelical Bishop James Jones to roll over was an absolute stroke of genius. You must send us a full report of how you did it. The Council will be most anxious to read your report. My how we love all that talk about David and Jonathan being lovers, Jesus and John being...OH THE BEST LINE EVER. Make sure that becomes part of the text for every future seminarian in every liberal seminary. From thoughtful speculation in a class room to the pulpit, is an easy road to walk. To undermine Him, at the very heart of their dreadful gospel, is music to our ears. We especially liked these lines of Jones..."One of them says literally that John was leaning against the bosom, breast, and chest of Jesus (kolpos). No English word or phrase fully captures the closeness of the liaison. On the cross Jesus makes his beloved friend his mother's son in an extraordinary covenant of love and on the day of the resurrection love propels the bereaved and beloved disciple to outrun Peter and arrive first at the tomb. Here is energizing love, spiritual emotional and physical." Make sure the PHYSICAL is emphasized. Keep sex to the forefront in all these discussions. Rowan Williams prevarications, now documented in that awful S.P.R.E.A.D. document, hints at similar sexual probabilities. Drive home the sexual dimension. Keep it high sounding and thoughtful but keep it there. Sooner or later, it will filter down to the masses who are largely indulging themselves anyway, but we want it heard in the pulpits where the faithful can be undermined.

I must tell you that the High Council chortled over the woman priestess declaring her love for Islam and wanting to have her cake and eat it, too, by remaining an Episcopal priest. She almost won the day. Have no fear she is firmly ours whether she returns to the Episcopal Church and to the priesthood or not.

Now I must say, what you achieved in the Los Angeles cathedral recently was a return to paganism of the best kind. Their horrible liturgy was replaced by idolatry and the worship of other gods. It would appear that you are achieving more than we could have hoped or asked for in such a short space of time. The rollover by these weak Episcopalians (and other denominations who will in time join them) will go down in the History of Hades as one of the great classic volumes of all eternity. Who would have thought that a return to the old paganism done up, of course, in fine garments and high sounding talk of diversity and love (a word we hate, but in this context sweet music to our ears), could have been achieved so swiftly?

Your moves in the Diocese of Pittsburgh were a brilliant stealth operation. How you managed to get 12 Vichy conservatives to turn on that horrible Duncan fellow with his bushy eyebrows and horrible humility will earn you a special embrace from Our Master. A special blood dessert will be offered at the High Table to capture that moment. You have learned the fine art of undermining the Other Side as few agents have achieved. Agent Slubnose did his work well. He too, will be rewarded for his educational methods.

The Anglican Communion Office must surely take the prize. The article in The Christian Challenge magazine, which said that the ACO leader Canon Kenneth Kearon allowed and even encouraged private same-sex blessings (wink, wink, nod, nod) while publicly saying it is not permissible, is precisely the kind of duplicity we aim for. Keep reminding them about who pays their bills. Katharine of Arrogant is a safe bet with the Episcopal Church check book. They will never bite the hand that feeds them. Both the TEC and the Canadian Anglican Church are safe in our father's bosom.

The High Priestess PB who let the cat out of the bag by saying that Vickie Gene Robinson was not the only partnered sodomite bishop she knows in TEC, nearly took the lid off the council. Bishop James

Pike was rolled out for the occasion and a pint of his blood made the rounds at High Table. We especially like all that talk about differing interpretations of their dreadful Scriptures. Now, that is the kind of spiritual chaos that you can teach the next group of agents we are training - Deviation 101.

The Eco-Archbishop is, of course, the grand prize. Get him to fudge more doctrines, suggesting that perhaps another line in the creed is unnecessary in order to join the church. If he can be made to say the cross was unnecessary (we doubt he would go for the child abuse argument) but something along the lines that God's love is so all pervasive that a mere acknowledgement of God's love only is necessary for salvation. Under no circumstances must talk of confession, repentance and newness of life (a truly horrible concept) ever leave his lips. It would be the kiss of death for us and life for them.

As for Lambeth itself, we deeply regret the orthodox will not be present. How much richer it would have been had they attended to witness the gang from Colin Coward's Changing Attitude plus 30 or more Integrity sodomites and lesbians from the United States, screaming inclusivity in the bishops faces while Gene is holding hands with his honeymoon partner - a photo op we will surely miss. In the meantime keep up the good work.

Your infernal father sends you his hottest greetings...

I remain your affectionate uncle,

Faust

SHARIA LAW AND THE ARCHBISHOP OF CANTERBURY

My dear Teufel,

The latest news out of England that the Archbishop of Canterbury wants to incorporate some aspects of Sharia Law into English Common Law is sweet music to our ears.

Our father took time out from his usual flame throwing to announce that everything was perfectly lining up for a major breakdown in Christendom with the Anglican Communion leading the way.

We, of course, have been working on the Methodists, Presbyterians, Lutherans, various Baptist groups, the NCC and WCC for years. - The ecumenical movement, with its Gadarene rush to water down all those hideous exclusive doctrines about Him, the atonement and all that ghastly business about celibacy before marriage and monogamy in marriage, has now effectively been discredited. The pansexual rollercoaster ride culminating in Gene Robinson's consecration in The Episcopal Church, has been the greatest news since Spong's 12 Theses.

Sadly, the Roman Catholic Church seems to be going in the opposite direction under that awful Pope Benedict fellow. When he clamped down on the Pink Mafia in their American seminaries, it was indeed a bad day for us. They cleaned out the sodomites. Mercifully, the Episcopal Church will open up their seminaries to them. That wonderful ex-Catholic sodomite and former Governor of New Jersey was a real coup for us.

The High Council applauds your noble efforts.

Of course, the unintended consequences of Rowan Williams' words are that it could backfire in the Global South, particularly in northern Nigeria where Islam is locked in a fierce battle with Christianity.

If there is an outbreak of violence and thousands of Anglican Christians die, it will make for a great martyrdom and intensify calls for Williams' resignation. Worse still, many new converts could flow from such killings. The blood of the martyrs is the seed of the church. We do not want this to happen.

As things now stand, Williams refuses to apologize for his remarks, arguing, as all intellectuals do, that they were taken out of context, and those weak-minded English bishops have no interest in a nasty ecclesiastical fight that would spill over into the press and Internet. Keep that besotted bishop of Southwark making inclusive noises about a press and media out of control, and then, in due course, paint Williams as the victim in this whole business. The Bishop of Oxford will come in handy for that. He loves the sounds of Islamic call to worship ringing in his and the nominal Anglicans ears at Oxford five times a day. It's enough to earn him an honorary doctorate from a formerly Christian college.

Keeping the Anglican Communion together so it falls still in one piece like Humpty Dumpty is the aim and objective, Teufel. Under no circumstances can there be schism.

Keep the Windsor Report alive and keep the Covenant going through a thousand nit picking changes. Make sure more committees, design teams, and more counsels are formed to keep everyone busy. Idle hands and all that can be dangerous. We all know, of course, that it all means nothing, but they don't know that. It keeps the folks at the Anglican Communion office in business doing nothing but stoking their own hell-bent fires as they finagle language so that The Episcopal Church and the Canadian Anglican Church can stay in the club.

Busyness is the key. Write much, keep reports being churned out which say little or nothing, but under no circumstances should there be any talk of their horrible life-changing gospel. That is the kiss of death for us and life for them. Talk of honoring their Baptismal vows (which they don't), baptismal covenants, and Open Communion will keep them distracted for many years.

The sociology of victimhood can be used greatly to our cause. Having those clergy in Australia recently, falling all over themselves apologizing to gays and marching (to their doom) in public, couldn't have been better.

The Bishop of Liverpool's recent mea culpa over sodomy was a thorough coup for us. Our father has ordered up a special medal for you to be given at the next Fires of Hell banquet, when next you appear.

You might, as a follow-up act, get Williams to attend a Scientology gabfest where he can appeal for funds for some ailing cathedral or some other charitable work on the basis, of course, that he put in a good word for Tom Cruise's latest movies, which the Archbishop of Canterbury can no doubt find and draw much spiritual enlightenment from.

Remember Teufel, the name of the game is deception, delay, deviance, and half-truths, but never outright lies. They are far too easy to spot.

You remain in our warmest embrace,

Your affectionate uncle,

Faust

BISHOP GENE PRAYS "TO THE GOD OF OUR MANY UNDERSTANDINGS"

My dear Teufel,

Hell is in hysterical ferment this week over the news that New Hampshire Episcopal Bishop Gene Robinson offered a generic prayer at President-Elect Obama's inauguration.

That his prayer should begin "to the God of our many understandings," acknowledging that no one Christian denomination nor any one faith tradition knows all there is to know about God, was sweet music to our Father's ears. That Robinson's microphone failed just as he begun was singularly bad luck. We suspect the Other Side deliberately sabotaged our good friend. No matter. It was a PR coup that he was up there in the first place promoting sodomy and his new inclusive god.

The more "understandings", the better, Teufel. He has abandoned the unique claims of Christ and soaked himself in the generic pool of ecumenical sludge that passes for interfaith understanding; precisely the kind of thing we want to encourage.

The adoration of Robinson by his adoring admirers almost reaches Adoration of the Magi proportion.

Keep all talk of faith vague and focus on words like "spirituality" and "many pathways to God" talk. Hell is paved with such pathways. It's all that talk about the "narrow way" leading to life eternal that needs to be trampled on and refuted.

The front-page article in the "New York Times" about a plane crashing in the Hudson River where people were heard to cry "Lord, forgive me my sins" as the plane went down is precisely the kind of thing we don't need. There are no atheists in fox holes as we all well know. It is precisely those kinds of moments that focus the mind on eternity. That is dangerous to our cause and mission. Plane crashes, wars and ships sinking never work to our advantage. People have time to repent.

Political changeovers, on the other hand, are grand occasions. Politicians and priests make great bedfellows. They strut around stages looking and sounding so self-important while the prayers religious folk offer up are as bland and generic as last week's news.

Assorted religions and prayers are like assorted bagels and worth about just as much.

As for the potential gay orgy in the Hilton Hotel in Washington, DC, http://americansfortruth.com/ at the time of the inauguration, whatever possessed you, if it was not our Father? Those kinds of things are quickly exposed through the Internet and start campaigns against it. The other side won and they closed it down. Those sort of overt behaviors are anathema to our way of thinking, Teufel. We do not want people to think in actual terms about sexual behaviors and the damage they cause. Those horrible statistics from the CDC, revealing that 65% of all venereal diseases come from homosexual men having anal intercourse, is information that must be suppressed. Spread disinformation and spread it fast. Blame such figures on homophobia. Get gays to blame the church for being uninclusive and causing these figures. When people allegedly feel excluded, they behave inappropriately. Put the blame squarely on heterosexuals. Do a lot of whining about feeling the pain of exclusion. UNDER NO CIRCUMSTANCES are men who engage in these sexual acts to shoulder the blame.

Those slogans lauding atheism on buses in England, and soon to be coming to Canada, are a disaster and stupid. All it does is rouse up the other side to mount a counter-offensive, with their announcement that a loving God actually cares about their vile lives. That tit for tat thing is stupid and serves no good purpose. See that it is stopped immediately.

Those sort of things make people THINK. That is exactly what we don't want them to do. When people get into jams, they naturally appeal to God or a higher power. That road might lead from atheism to theism and then on to a personal God and all that dreadful talk of sin and salvation. Look what happened to C. S. Lewis for Hell's sake. This sloganeering campaign is a disaster and it must end. Make it so.

Teufel, you must subvert more clandestinely. Focus on the sins of greed and fear. Keep people worrying about bombs falling and buildings blowing up. Let them think that when banks fail and the stock market continues to crash, their lives will be destroyed forever. Keep them thinking about this world, not the next. Let them think that the economy is their source of strength and that whatever God is out there, is not. Destroy all that mushy talk about love of neighbor, a vile idea put out by the other side.

Keep people doubting. Doubt is good. If people start thinking that they have actually found and then come to the truth, fill their minds with a false humility that such absolutist thinking and talk is arrogance and fundamentalist.

You can never overwork that word fundamentalist too much, Teufel. Never mind that all it means is that there are certain fundamentals of their wretched faith. We have turned the word to great psychological advantage. From a noun to a nasty verb, we can label anybody who thinks they might know the truth as being fundamentalist. What delicious irony there is in this, Teufel.

In the Episcopal Church, the revisionists are focusing on canons and constitutions. They have become the real FUNDAMENTALISTS, but no one seems to have noticed. Keep the remnant orthodox cowed and humiliated, any time they rear their heads and talk about not being included.

We want them included, but only to an extent. The revisionists need a remnant to beat up on so they can feel good about themselves. If there were none, it would be a loss for our side. Continue the humiliation over women's ordination and sodomy always holding out the carrot of compromise along with the stick of mandatory conformity. In time, they will either roll over or get out.

That dreadful Iker fellow is one smart cookie. He has covered his bases well with that Canon 32 which has the deep thinkers in New York wetting their collective legal knickers. Undermine him, Teufel. That is an order. Find their weakness and exploit it.

That Katie Sherrod woman in the Diocese of Ft. Worth is a clever writer and perfect for our side. She has the right degree of faux outrage and moral snobbery. Make sure she joins forces with the lesbian priestess Susan Russell, an admirable woman for our side. Let them vent their outrage on orthodox believers. Make sure they damn them, accuse them, curse them, snarl at them, but then at the end offer up soft words of reconciliation to keep the orthodox at the table. This has been your special genius, which our Father has duly noted.

Continue to keep the masses iPod ears filled with sounds of music, mindless gossip and Hollywood trivia. They must have every moment filled with noise. Do not let them think, unless it is about money, sex or power.

It was a wonderful coup of yours to make sure the Hollywood elites have their own religion in Scientology. Special people demand special attention. Pansexuality is slowly, but surely, killing The Episcopal Church and will, in time, course through the veins of the entire Anglican Communion.

The revisionists have become the instruments of their own oppression helped along by you.

Our "joy" will be complete when you have completed your mission. Hell will be filled with "many understandings". Do not lose heart, Teufel.

You remain in our warmest embrace,

Your affectionate uncle,

Faust

VICTORY AT GENERAL CONVENTION

My dear Teufel,

Word of your enormous success has reached our father's ears. What you achieved in Anaheim at GC2009 this past week was beyond our wildest imaginings.

That you should have obtained a public confession from that Jefferts Schori woman that personal faith or conversion of any sort was unnecessary and was actually a Western heresy must surely go down in the annals of hellish history as a first.

We have atheists and agnostics, unbelievers and disbelievers, but to have someone actually masquerading as a Christian and publicly denying one of its central tenets is a feat of uncommon performance. You are to be congratulated.

Your success at undermining that vile religion so adroitly through a female leader, (equality has its plusses) no less, only proves our point that heretics who rise through the ranks of the priestly classes only aid and abet our side. Jefferts Schori is the apogee of the feminist and pansexual revolution roaring through the churches of the West. Spong is her alter ego. Our success in undermining mainline churches like The Episcopal Church with pansexual acceptance and then calling it a "justice" issue rather than a moral issue deftly deflects it away from the truth that it will ultimately destroy their souls making them all hell bound. Heaven's loss, Hell's gain.

Our father has placed the highest priority on undermining Western Christianity. The successes achieved this week in The American Episcopal Church will undoubtedly be followed by more of the same with the Lutherans, Presbyterians, United Church of Christ, Moravians and, in time, and a lot of effort on your part, the United Methodists.

The thin end of the wedge has penetrated the heart of the Christian behemoth; you will continue to hammer it home, opening up more fractures here and there till we have swallowed them all up. They will, in time, be ripe, for our ultimate goal - the triumph of Islam and the imposition of Sharia Law.

Let them cry out for justice for all oppressed peoples, but make sure that any talk of "justice" for orthodox types is glossed over with talk that when they were in charge, they gave nothing to the other side. Now it is their turn to hold the crown of victory. Never mind that the cry of repentance for all peoples was undermining OUR cause. It is important to focus away from any such talk and on to the whine of inclusion, diversity and justice for all peoples.

Keep the Listening Process alive and well. Make sure they get millions of dollars to listen themselves to death over sodomite inclusion. It all works in our favor.

Add to all this the undermining of Western morality with abortion, Internet porn, divorce, the abandonment of children, further undermining of the educational system, preaching moral relativity (keep the pressure on homosexual acceptance in the schools) and the rejection of absolute truth ...and our work will almost be done.

That lesbian Ragsdale woman at Episcopal Divinity School preaching that abortion is a blessing was further sweet music to our ears. It is emptying their churches faster than we could have hoped or imagined.

Now it is very important, Teufel, to keep the institution alive. To do so, you must keep the remaining orthodox dioceses and parishes in TEC. If they leave, TEC will wilt and die even faster. If The Episcopal Church dies, and on its present trajectory it most certainly will, then it will be apparent to everyone. That will only undermine our cause. Whatever you do, keep it going, if only to make their case (and ours) that this church is where it is at - the seeker friendly church, the inclusive church, the emergent church, full of new ideas, taking the e-word (evangelism) and giving it a whole new definition and meaning.

The thing is not to kill off the church, but to undermine it from within, to change the definition of things, making words mean the opposite of what they originally meant and keeping people seduced by the language of inclusion. Keep the empty shells of churches and cathedrals open if only for tourism traffic. The English have that down to a fine art.

Keep Robinson smiling and hopping from one event to the next while making sure he stays off the booze. Keep him going to AA and announcing he now believes in a "higher power". Good stuff that changes nothing. Hell is filled with people who believe in a higher power. His upcoming appearance at Greenbelt, England, is a major coup. There he will preach his inclusive god and seductive gospel that embraces all manner of sexualities. The only sexual "sin" left in The Episcopal Church is heterosexual adultery. We need to trot that out occasionally to remind the world that TEC still has standards. (Grin)

Marriage, that horrid institution that has provided so much stability for societies and cultures for centuries, must be undermined. If not, then it must be twisted to meet the new sexual realities of the world and church. With your able assistance, we have taken it out of the sphere of heterosexual behavior and procreation, and have turned it into a narcissistic, self-absorbed past-time. Keep pushing the issue of ersatz rights - rights for gays, rights for women, rights for the transgendered, rights for same-sex marriage, and rights for dogs, if need be. Let them keep talking about the "other", but under no circumstances must this talk move into an understanding of a transcendent "other" - of a loving G-d who demands obedience and faith.

Keep that Jefferts Schori woman well supplied with heresies. Above all, keep her focused on this worldly transformation. Under no circumstances must she be given a glimpse of another world, a heavenly realm, a kingdom not made with hands...keep her believing that MDGs will change the world making it a better place with heaven just an extension of this world as SHE knows it.

Your work has been masterful, Teufel. Our father broke open a pint of Pike's blood the other evening just to celebrate your incredible success.

Let the darkness roll on.

You remain in our warmest embrace,

Your affectionate uncle,

Faust

CHURCH OF ENGLAND ALLIANCES WITH SODOMITES

My dear Teufel,

Your successes keep piling on top of each other like so much excrement following a gay pride parade day.

The Council of Hades met this past week in emergency session and was positively stunned to learn of your new initiatives in The Church of England.

The momentum gained at the recent Episcopal General Convention for full pansexual acceptance is now being carried over into open spiritual warfare in the Church of England. Well done.

What fools the British have become; their society is slowly sinking beneath the waves of political correctness, assisted suicide, moral laxity, family disintegration, the rehashing of old socialist theories, and, slow but sure, invasion by Islam and Sharia Law. Now the full acceptance of pansexual behavior has hit the Church of England, courtesy of its American counterpart. This surely ranks as the high point of the week and, hopefully, can be made to fester for months to come. The final undermining of Western Christianity, particularly in the Anglican Communion, has begun in earnest.

I must confess to you that the Council is in total awe of your achievements and was reduced to stunned silence observing two minutes of evil thoughts to commemorate your gains. Evil shouts and cries of glee were later heard all over Hell.

It seems to us that the alliance of sodomite organizations in England, led by that Changing Attitude crowd (I doubt we could have achieved such nomenclature) , was brilliant in and of itself but that you forced disarray among evangelicals who could not totally agree on the issue or find a strategy or counter-offensive was masterful. FULCRUM writers have become the masters of evangelical agit-prop. Disarray is a brilliant strategy. Dividing over who should run what and where and the final drafting of this or that statement with more caveats than tooth fillings is a stroke of genius.

Make sure Church of England evangelical bishops keep silent, sow the seeds of clubbiness and containment so they won't feel the cold winds of rejection by their fellow bishops should they actually have to stand up and say that sodomy defiles the body and casts them out of their vile kingdom and into outer darkness...and into our embrace. Under no circumstances must they coalesce into a formidable body that challenges the status quo.

I must tell you, however, that the council is very worried by this Fellowship of Confessing Anglicans (FCA) crowd. They even got the

Queen's endorsement though that might be just a pro forma matter. It does indicate that the spiritual war is heating up and you must undermine it, Teufel. The Queen must never say what she really thinks, only to offer platitudes about being committed to the Anglican Church etc. etc.

Any notion of a real coalition of those vile Global South fundamentalist bishops and archbishops from GAFCON and that new vile coalition in North America (AC-NA), led by that bushy-eyed geek Duncan, with FCA coming up the rear (I wish it was so) poses a major road block. If they form a super structure next to Rowan and Lambeth Palace, all our work will be for naught.

It is important that the academic evangelicals start raising road blocks and focusing on minutiae, Teufel. Let them parse the meaning of words and sentences from statements that might otherwise be clear to ordinary lay folk. Let them pick the Ridley-Cambridge Draft to death and keep parsing Article 4 till it falls off the table. Ephraim Radner is totally incomprehensible after the second sentence. Make sure he works on the final draft. Absolutely no one will know what he is talking about, neither will we, but who the hell cares, if you'll pardon the pun.

Alarm bells went off here when the Bishop of Durham, Tom Wright almost achieved clarity with a statement following the American general convention. He was actually comprehensible, not only to his fellow bishops, but to the church's clergy and laity. This was a disastrous moment. His words are still reverberating around the communion and ordinary people are catching on. He even caught the Archbishop of Canterbury off guard.

At the end of the day, Teufel, he must offer palliative words of comfort to Rowan. Under no circumstances can there be a rift between these two men. The loss of Bishop Michael Nazir-Ali indicated a potentially a major rift in their HOB. Now you must move to silence him forever. No more media coverage. He must sink without trace.

Whatever happens now, Teufel, there must be no courageous clarity from Evangelicals, and all the orthodox. There are evangelical leaders, including evangelical bishops, who want to "resist" the erosion of orthodox faith and practice, but they must be made to believe in the institution above all else. Keep many of them thinking that a House of Lords appointment awaits some of them...that Queen and country and keeping the Church of England together is a higher notion than all that talk of sin and judgment, redemption and grace and a kingdom yet to come and G-d dwelling in temples (read cathedrals) not made with hands. Focus them on the visible, on the here and now. Under no circumstances are they to catch a glimpse of something far greater; that would undermine everything.

It is they, above all, who have the power to steady the ship and, (to mix metaphors), settle the flock. That must not happen.

Those horrid uninclusive words "Choose you this day ..." works for our side too, Teufel. Never forget that.

The Council embraces you. Our father embraces you,

I remain your affectionate uncle,

Faust

VICTORY FOR BISHOP JOHN SHELBY SPONG

My dear Teufel,

So that Spong fellow has finally claimed victory for the pansexualists. http://tinyurl.com/nw9ge5

What a gem he has proven to be. As you know, he has been firmly lodged in our camp for nearly four decades. It is to his credit that Spong has lived long enough to see his success in the triumph of sodomy and the inevitable destruction of The Episcopal Church, along with such lay luminaries as Louie Crew and other sodomite advocators from Integrity and the much married bishops Walter Righter, Gene Robinson and Otis Charles.

Let them exalt in their victory, Teufel. They are ours. Let them shout it from every inclusive pulpit, every newspaper and every talk show host who will grovel before them in secular obeisance. It is ours to watch and ours to chortle.

It is a triumph for which our father will duly reward you. You have done sterling work. Seal the deal, if you can, by making sure that another sodomite or lesbian is elected bishop of Los Angeles or Minnesota. It doesn't really matter who; the important thing is to finally force the hand of Jefferts Schori in her dealings with Rowan Williams.

If one is elected, she will be forced to admit that Resolution B033 is dead on arrival. Then she will also be forced to admit that resolutions D025 and C056 were not merely descriptive, as she said in a letter to Williams, but prescriptive. Then she will have to decide whether she will be the chief consecrator at their consecrations or not.

Remind her of what Frank Griswold did. He told the Primates in 2003 he would never consecrate an avowed sodomite to the episcopacy. Three weeks later, he went ahead and did just that saying he had no control over how individual diocesan bishops and the HOB vote. The result was Gene Robinson. Oh what history he has made, and how many tens of thousands of Episcopal simpletons he has pushed into our camp.

Keep the lies and prevarications coming, Teufel. Keep the orthodox believing (what few are left) that there are still more lines in the sand to be drawn and that they should stay in TEC as the church's loyal opposition.

The most important thing is making sure that Rowan Williams believes in TEC and its future, and that his two track or two-tier solution is the answer to keeping the Anglican Communion together.

Williams' brilliance at fudge should not go unrecognized. Sooner or later, the fudge will turn into goo and melt into our arms. Make sure some seminary or other gives him an honorary doctorate for keeping everyone at the table. Hell is filled with brilliant academics who know more than G-d.

Keep the Listening Process alive. Find some liberal philanthropist who will drop another million dollars or two into the Listening pot. Let them listen themselves to death, Teufel. They are ours. Any thought of sexual mutability must be upheld forever and the whine and faux pain pansexualists feel must also be recorded forever and parked in the annals of hell.

Keep the notion alive and well that talk of exclusion is narrow-minded and fundamentalist. Conversely, the word inclusion is a powerful word that we want kept alive. Any talk of some being in or out of their wretched kingdom must be against an all loving, all embracive G-d who wants all to be saved and will ultimately save all. Ditto for diversity.

Make sure liberal seminaries abandon all talk of substitutionary atonement. Make sure the language of inclusion is embedded so deep in their studies that they leave the seminaries complete converts to our side. That new homosexual convert to Episcopalianism (from the vile Roman Catholic Church) Jim McGreevey, the former Governor of NJ, is a real catch. He should be elevated immediately and fast tracked to a bishopric. A handsome sodomite...he and Gene will make an attractive pair appearing on talk show hosts across the nation. If you can possibly elevate a bi-sexual to the Episcopal priesthood make sure his or her first sermon reads, "Going Both Ways" a reflection on Peter, James and John.

Keep making the point that sexuality issues are about "justice" not morality. Push the line that morality is malleable and not fixed and keep the pansexualists arguing that the Global South has polygamy (a myth by the way but worth perpetuating) and therefore the West should be entitled to sodomy. It's a great quid pro quo. Also, make sure that the pansexualists keep trotting out those Old Testament texts prohibiting certain meats even though these ceremonial laws have nothing to do with HIS damnable fixed laws on human biology and behavior.

We do so love nomenclature that begins with... "The church commends sexual relationships that are 'trustworthy,' 'loving,' 'fulfilling,' 'committed,' and 'nurturing.'" These suggest that some homosexual and other non-marital relationships might satisfy these criteria. Of course they do, Teufel. These are all touchy feely words, that have nothing to do with objective truth and that is the point. Keep any talk of revealed truth from these people. They must believe that their G-d has changed His mind for them and they must believe it with fervor and passion.

That statement of Spong's the other day that G-d is not personal, but an extension of ourselves should be written over every church portal.

What is so compelling is that the "Christian" churches are doing it all for us. You simply pushed the pain of exclusion button and they started racing our way. We note with levity that the Lutherans seem headed down the same sewer over pansexuality as the Episcopalians. The Quakers rolled over recently. Excellent work.

I must confess to you, Teufel, we have not had this much success since those great but horrible revivals of the 18th century that pushed millions into the camp of the righteous. With post-modernism, we have undone most of it, but still there remain pockets of resistance to us.

Make sure that liberal and revisionist Episcopal bishops destroy orthodox priests in their dioceses. We do not merely want their properties with them gone, but we want them destroyed and imprisoned, if at all possible. If you can get those wretched righteous priests, Don Armstrong and Matt Kennedy, doing time for allegedly fiddling their books, it will arm the revisionists with more ammunition. But watch out for the backlash, do NOT make martyrs of them. It could backfire on us.

What we ultimately want to do is have the whole mainline Protestant experience to embrace sexual revisionism. In doing so, it would deliberately sideline itself. It would exalt western liberal notions of individual moral autonomy above shared understandings of the Bible. It would also alienate the majority of its own members. We want the whole lot of them heading down the road to theological marginalization, internal division, accelerating membership loss, and cultural irrelevance.

Our goal is their full and total destruction. Hell awaits them.

I remain your affectionate uncle,

Faust

THE LISTENING PROCESS

My dear Teufel,

Word of your enormous success with America's mainline denominations continues to draw our father's attention and gratitude.

That you are systematically undermining them all over pansexual behavior is nothing short of genius. We note with interest that the Scandinavian countries have been seduced by sodomy as well, indicative of that fact that deviant sex can be sold trans nationally especially in Luther's denomination. It has taken nearly 500 years, but we are almost there. We were never able to undo or undermine Simul Justus Et Peccatore, but we did it with Copulo ergo sum. Sex is the new salvation.

We are particularly delighted that America's premier denomination, The Episcopal Church, has almost completely rolled over. Only a handful of Communion Partner bishops remain and I am sure you will see to it that replacements in dioceses like Springfield and Western Kansas will see moderate men of all shades of opinion claiming the high moral ground of theological inclusivity. No screaming faggots, of course, no Mary Glasspools or Gene Robinsons, just a modest, contemplative, happily married photogenic liberal who promises to bring everybody to the table to have "conversation." They are the best kind. They are, of course, firmly in our camp, but don't know it. Make sure they are men who know how to listen. Oh my, how we love that word.

"Listening" and "conversation" have been the most manipulative verbal tools at our disposal to woo and win fence sitters and alleged orthodox types.

That the Listening Process still continues with pots of money to keep it all going, enabled by a queer Episcopal priest was a stroke of luck. Make sure that for every ex gay they "listen" to, that the voices and "pain" of 20 "marginalized" homosexuals is fed into the system. Remember, Teufel, the art of seduction is best done by desensitizing and ultimately dumbing down the other side so they finally just roll over and accept this abominable behavior that has brought so many to our father's hell.

We particularly like the fact that the Archbishop of Canterbury calls on all sides to continue listening and to be in "conversation" with one another. This is a great strategy, almost as good as listening. Its intent is to converse and converse and converse till everybody gets worn down and finally rolls over. It was the strategy of Frank Griswold. It worked brilliantly for him among the House of Bishops, it is working brilliantly for us.

I must confess to you Teufel that the rollover of this Bishop Jones fellow in the Church of England recently was an unexpected serendipitous moment. A leading evangelical bishop no less. What fools they are Teufel. The new argument that sexuality is a second-tier issue is sweet music to our ears and fills hell with those who believe they can divorce spirituality from sexual behavior.

That Global South archbishops and bishops hardened their hearts against us and formed their horrid GAFCON was a bitter blow, but fear not, Teufel. Our emissaries and agents are hard at work in Uganda and Nigeria, in the latter fomenting Islamic fanatics to kill Christians though there is a danger that could backfire. We are working daily to undermine their dogmatic stance. We are throwing around the word "homophobia" like so much sand in the faces of their bishops. We are also doing our utmost to undermine the African courts, sending in our political agents in the form of UN representatives and that dreadful creature from America, Hilary Clinton. What a godsend she has been, if you'll pardon the pun.

On reviewing your successes, Teufel, we would urge you to lighten up on the litigation front. All is not going well there.

The other side has had singular successes in South Carolina and, it would appear, Virginia. Nothing is set in stone and we have appeals out there, but we urge caution as this could all backfire on us. If any State Supreme Court sees in favor of the other side, it sets a legal precedent and makes our case to The Supreme Court of the United States even harder to forever enshrine the Dennis Canon. Mind how you go, Teufel, our father is watching your progress.

As it seems almost assured that the Diocese of Los Angeles will have a lesbian for a bishop, make sure that the voices of the Windsor bishops and Communion Partner bishops are heard to say that they want to remain in communion with the Archbishop of Canterbury. It is imperative that the Communion stays together in order for us to undermine the whole thing, Teufel. Splits and separations do us no good; they highlight the differences, create martyrs and embolden evangelists and church planters.

Rowan Williams must be made to hear that holding onto The Episcopal Church is imperative if only for the sake of the dwindling Communion Partner bishops and their dioceses.

Keep working on Williams and his people to create wedges among soft Global South archbishops, bishops and theologians with endless encounters and theological position papers. Wherever there is a perceived weakness in Southeast Asia or Africa, exploit it, Teufel.

We were delighted to read of the recent Communique from the Dialogue of African and Canadian Bishops in England. Such gatherings are sweet music to our ears. Putting together five Canadian and six African dioceses and engaging them in diocese-to-diocese theological dialogue on matters relating to human sexuality and mission was a stroke of genius. We especially love this little phrase: "As we continue to learn about each other's mission contexts, cultures, values and languages, each of us grows in deeper mutual understanding of theological and ethical positions - both our own and those of our partners."

As post-modernity overtakes Africa and Asia, as it surely will, these "dialogues" will win them over to our side, Teufel. Endless discussion and conversation ALWAYS works in our favor. As long as no fool stands up and says, "this is the Word of the Lord" (theologians rarely do that, only prophets), then we will slowly but surely seduce them all. Indaba them to death, Teufel.

We can't help but notice the irony that the Anglican Church of Canada is slowly sinking into the sunset with whole dioceses like Quebec and British Columbia on the brink of going out of business. To think that they send theologians to talk to the Africans whose dioceses and provinces are growing by the millions about "mission contexts, culture, values...and ethical positions." Our father was heard to scream with evil laughter when he heard the news.

However, having said this, we are concerned about what we hearing about goings on in the Diocese of South Carolina. If you are not careful, Teufel, you will make Bishop Mark Lawrence into a martyr for orthodoxy.

Ms. Jefferts Schori has very little on him except a lot of hearsay and the other side is getting better, smarter and more aggressive lawyers. Long gone are the days of pro bono legal half-wits. These damned lawyers actually get together and talk. They know more, file more appeals and they are fighting back with everything they have got. Mind how you go, Teufel. Nothing is sure in dioceses like Ft. Worth, San Joaquin, Pittsburgh and Quincy and the outcomes are by no means certain. In the meantime, ACNA and that vile Duncan fellow have taken the upper hand with his new province and a call to plant 1000 churches. Our father is furious.

The race is won not by the swiftest, Teufel, it is won by the persistent. Many on the other side have developed serious spinal columns that we would never have guessed. This is especially so among women, where we have seen a sudden rise in interest and fight-back. Who would have thought it, Teufel? On the other hand, the Presiding Bishop of TEC is a dream for us. Her words last summer at General Convention denying personal faith in Jesus had our father briefly wordless.

Our father hails your efforts, but we must never forget that the other side has huge resources at its disposal. Keep undermining them, Teufel. Your reward and a senior place in our father's kingdom are assured. Retirement is out of the question.

I remain your affectionate uncle,

Faust

EPISCOPAL PRESIDING BISHOPS JEFFERTS SCHORI PUTS ARCHBISHOP ROWAN WILLIAMS IN HIS PLACE

My dear Teufel,

It would appear to our father's inner circle of courtly devils that this Jefferts Schori woman's recent baring of her fangs to Rowan Williams was a kairos moment in the life of the Anglican Communion. That she did it so publicly and not behind closed doors in the back rooms of Lambeth Palace or at a closed door primatial gathering is something to cherish. We are more than just a little amused. In fact, you might say our father was positively gleeful. He sipped an entire goblet of Pike's blood.

Her predecessor, Frank (of the flexible wrist) Griswold, was never so public except for one of his "private" outbursts in Dromantine at Rowan Williams over his refusal to stand up to Nigerian Primate Peter Akinola over homosexual acceptance that was leaked by that dreadful VOL reporter. For the most part, Griswold publicly parsed and spun what was going on behind closed doors to make his Episcopal garden look free of heretical weeds. It wasn't of course, as we know, but this Jefferts Schori is something else. What an absolute treasure. One thinks perhaps they might have picked her right off the bottom of the ocean floor for the job.

When they elected her Presiding Bishop, we knew she was truly on our father's side, but we never thought, in our wildest dreams (and trust me our father's nightmares can be heard for miles around), that she would come this far (and not be faithful) so fast.

Her rip at Rowan over this miter business was a stupid bit of nonsense, but she managed to morph it into an issue of the victimization of women...truly a gem; a sort of Murder in the Cathedral by mitre. She meted to the wannabe women bishops' issue in England a colossal hand up and an open door of victimhood. All those embarrassing questions about the exclusion of gays and lesbians from all orders of ministry she and her Executive Council posed to Secretary General Canon Kenneth Kearon just ratcheted up the pain a whole lot more. What a week it has truly been.

Kearon left Maryland whipped. He deserved it, of course. As one blogger rightly pointed out, when the revisionists no longer have the orthodox to kick around, they turn on their own and devour them. Our father worked on this strategy for a long time, Teufel, in one his famous seminars on "Winning through Intimidation". He has honed it into "Winning by Victimization." You will recall that Joseph Stalin was his most famous disciple with the former. "Turning on your Own" came in a later series of lectures. "Winning by Desensitization", especially in this "Listening Process" for pansexual acceptance, might well be his highest achievement.

It would also appear that there is much weakness in the Church of England's armor these days, Teufel, over sodomy that is worth exploiting.

The list of "wobbler" bishops now runs to Liverpool, Gloucester, Chelmsford, Manchester, Lichfield and Stafford, but doubtless more could be included. They are all Rowan's men and, therefore, ours. Push harder, Teufel. Make them look vaguely courageous and, at the same time, humble about admitting their homophobia. A touch of contriteness helps...and for hell's sake, make sure the TV cameras are on when they go public with their "confession". A picture is worth...etc.

The wonderful news is that Rowan just doesn't get it. The more he tries to find compromises to hold the whole Anglican Communion together, the faster it falls apart. We know where his true sympathies lie, of course, and that makes it all the more interesting and devilish.

The Covenant is really quite farcical. The orthodox happily sign on to it while the liberals and revisionists prevaricate because they don't like Section 4, which is really quite toothless. The truth is, any sanction of their behavior is cause for alarm with cries of homophobia from organizations like Changing Attitude and Integrity and Jefferts Schori.

Schori is busy, we note from you, running around the world Schoring up her pansexual base among liberal Anglican provinces. A brilliant move on your part, Teufel. Keep her flying and talking, and talking...and talking about (homo)sex till her miter falls off. We did note, with alarm, that they banned her in Christchurch Cathedral (NZ), no doubt to keep Rowan happy, or at least not totally apoplectic.

Rowan's private views on homosexuality which, we know, are at variance with his public stand so as not to offend the Global South, is coming back to bite him in the proverbial bottom. The truth is the Global South is not buying his theological schizophrenia, any more. They are quietly distancing themselves from him.

We believe it is time, Teufel, for you to put the thumbscrews on Rowan the Compromiser, to smoke him out, force him into the open. If you don't, there will be all Hell to pay. As long as he thinks he is finding a way forward, the orthodox will just keep drifting away, forming their own more perfect union. The sight of ACNA, GAFCON and then FCA along with four fleeing Episcopal dioceses and some 800 parishes in the US and Canada is not something we bargained on and it has created enormous foment in the nether regions. Our father has been breathing fire and brimstone ever since that dreadful Duncan fellow started making orthodox waves. That he has been hedged about with so much spiritual protection has been an issue of profound angst to our father.

Jefferts Schori might split the communion, or, at a minimum, polarize it to the point of irrelevancy. She has killed off evangelism in her own church, but this in turn has forced the Global South to be more aggressive in their evangelistic efforts. Keep up the pressure on Islam to bash sodomy in the West. It will also give them the excuse they need to persecute Christians in the Global South.

Finally, and this is most important Teufel, focus on corrupting language. Make words mean something from what they originally meant. Think Alice in Wonderland:

"When I use a word," Humpty Dumpty said, in a rather scornful tone, "it means just what I choose it to mean - neither more nor less."

"The question is," said Alice, "whether you can make words mean so many different things."

"The question is," said Humpty Dumpty, "which is to be master - that's all."

Take for instance, the latest word game played by a certain Richard Helmer in an essay he wrote over the meaning of "Chastity".

In times past, chastity meant abstinence that is refraining from sexual activity outside of marriage between a man and a woman (It is important to stress the latter now that gay marriage is out and about.). This was the gold standard throughout church history and still is for most of the world especially the Global South.

Helmer refers to chastity, which, he says, has to do with "fidelity". Then he says, "Chastity means setting aside dominance and control and seeking instead a new way to relate to the world and to God. He then goes on to say he is concerned about "a failure of chastity" which he then clarifies this way: "...I don't mean sex outside the marriage. By chastity in marriage I mean the challenge of setting aside the stubborn drive to control or change the person we most cherish."

He then added, "Chaste behavior has been in the quiet but transformative story-telling and building up of authentic relationships across the divides of gender, class, race, culture, sexuality, and ideology all across the Communion recently. Chastity allows us to be ourselves by allowing others to be themselves. Chastity makes it known when we are encountering oppression and articulates our needs as they arise. Chastity seeks honest accountability. Chastity sets aside the weapons and metaphors of war for an honest, authentic justice. Chastity endeavors to shed the harbored resentments and unmet wants of our brief lives and move forward in renewed relationship."

The subtlety of this, Teufel, is to lift all sexual restraints in the name of chastity. This is brilliant. Stay away from words like abstinence, or virginity (heaven forbid, if you'll pardon the pun). Helmer has abandoned Scripture (much to our father's liking) and opts for a Gnostic, sociological interpretation of chastity that allows homosexuals to advance their behavior in the name of not being oppressed and being free.

How can bishops Gene Robinson or Mary Glasspool possibly be chaste? A man or a woman in a same sex relationship cannot possibly be chaste. It is a contradiction in terms.

They must not be made to see this, Teufel. We love all that talk of "mutuality" and "faithfulness" and "encouragement" and "life enhancement"... these words are sweet music to our ears. Any talk of chastity as abstinence or obedience to THEIR Father must be thwarted at every turn.

The saying that hell hath no fury like Jefferts Schori scorned pales against our father whose fury knows no bounds if he should catch even a whiff of repentance from those who have sworn eternal fealty to us. There would be all hell to pay.

I remain your affectionate uncle,

Faust

PENNSYLVANIA BISHOP CHARLES BENNISON RETURNS TO THE FOLD

My dear Teufel,

Word of the glorious return of Charles E. Bennison to the Diocese of Pennsylvania reached our father's ears and none too soon. We were growing tired of hearing about the rapid growth of the Anglican Church in North America and He was growing quite discouraged that the break-up of the Anglican Communion could spell the end of all that talk about "conversation" and "listening" and "inclusion" and "diversity" and "generous orthodoxy."

Such words are the "daily bread" of our father.

Then came word that Charles (AKA Chuckles) Bennison was returning once again to the Episcopal fold. Our father and his counsel of devils positively roiled in mirth for hours, mocking The Sociopathic One and just braying that he would continue the diocese on its downward spiral. We do wonder what the other side was really thinking when they threw the wolf back in among the sheep. It is hard to know how we could exactly mimic that or create a situation more perfect to our liking.

He will persecute the remaining faithful, abuse women emotionally and, because they fear losing their jobs, they will take it lying down, if you'll pardon the pun. In time he will make the diocese look like the last days of Sodom and Gomorrah. If a secretary should happen to pass his office and hear him singing a verse of "Blessed Assurance Jesus is Mine" please make sure they call the white coats and have him carted off.

The self-destructiveness of Episcopal Church leaders is hard to fathom even by our standards. From Vickie Gene Robinson to Mary Glasspool, they keep throwing themselves off the cliff face in droves. They do so much harm to themselves that it requires very little from us to make them roll over. In fact, they seem to WANT to roll over and jump right into hell. They do it with so much double talk and high-sounding phrases like this choice morsel: "Instead of debating the covenant, then, I believe we would better spend our time rebuilding the foundation -- laying aside our rigid positions and stereotypes of the "other side" in favor of authentic dialogue. Then, when we have made significant progress in that direction, we can reconsider the covenant, this time as an affirmation of our restored bonds of affection."

This kind of claptrap, compromise language and endless talk of dialogue thrills our hearts. We want them to dialogue themselves to death, spiritual death that is, with no hope of redemption. They reject the Law of Non-Contradiction in favor of a watered-down, wishy-washy, "why can't we all stay together" mantra that has our father in stitches.

We are delighted to see that the Diocese of Springfield has whittled its field of candidates down to three, none of whom pose a serious threat to us. We would prefer the Stevenson fellow. He is so ambitious and a team player to boot. He is very much to our liking. See that he gets the nod. We will have so much fun watching the orthodox get betrayed...one more time.

The newly reinvigorated Anglican Consultative Council with its near total liberal takeover was a stroke of genius. That Secretary General Kearon fellow is very much to our liking -- an institutionalist wonk and a moderate man of all shades of opinion but always to the left. He's a real charmer, flatterer and loser, the perfect man for the job. He's recovered well from his bout in Maryland with the TEC liberal leadership and is firmly back in the saddle just in time to kiss Jefferts Schori's checkbook and the rest of the liberal appartiks in London. That Asian attorney briefly upset the applecart with his broadside, but we feel sure he will resign like the orthodox Anglican Archbishops leaving the field wide open for Kearon to fill the void with institutional appartiks and revisionists.

Which brings me to the main thrust of my note to you, Teufel.

We have a strong sense that the Anglican Communion is truly coming apart at the seams with Rowan Williams unable to hold it together for much longer. Women's Ordination will undo the Church of England. Sodomy will continue to beat at Lambeth Palace doors with the Evangelicals and Anglo-Catholics looking for sanctuary and refuge elsewhere. Pansexuality has the Global South theologically and emotionally unglued.

We have loved state churches. Their religion is as phony as a Timex watch hit by a light rapid transit train. Countries across Europe that have tied church and state together in an unholy alliance have always been sweet music to our ears.

Modern trendy culture with a large dollop of Islamic Fundamentalism will in time topple them all. They have all confused that beastly kingdom talk by Him with nationalistic, utopian visions of a revived state Christianity. We hear that the Russian Orthodox Church is once again reviving itself as a state religion to make people moral. Keep them on the path to reviving the state with a veneer of religion but keep them from the Man of Nazareth and reading the New Testament for themselves. On no account must faith be seen as personal. Keep the religious institutions and churches going by all and any means. See that they prosper, but on no account must they talk of faith in any meaningful terms. Luther, Calvin, Cranmer, Ryle, Ridley, the Wesleys, Graham and others have done it with terrible losses to our side. Any revival of faith in Him would amount to a catastrophe of the worst order.

Mind how you destroy it, Teufel; do it carefully, slowly and with deliberation. Any sign of a revived faith must be nipped in the bud immediately. Remember to use jealousy and slander of godly people as a weapon. The Internet has done wonders for our side in this respect. Destroy character as quickly as possible with innuendo and, if that doesn't work, with outright lies.

We are particularly enamored with the British approach to anyone who opposes sodomy and wears their faith around their necks. Individuals are losing their jobs. In time, they will go to jail for opposing what the state, and, by its silence, what the church now embraces. However, mind how you go, Teufel, it could backfire.

The most important thing you can do is to create a counterfeit faith that mimics the real thing but is not faith at all. Keep up the appearance of things. Let the religious leaders talk about morality, the environment, women's ordination, but keep them from entering into a personal faith that trusts solely in Him who lived and died for them. On no account must they entertain such thoughts.

Hammer justice for all, peace in our time, no fear of Islam, justice for gays, women, wombats and whales, if need be. Under no circumstances should they be allowed to reflect on the Sermon on the Mount or meditate on John Chapter 1 or the book of Colossians and the exaltation of The One who was before all time and in whom everything co-inheres. We cannot bear a repeat of the "darker" side of history.

We have almost won the Culture Wars, Teufel. Individual battles over sodomite acceptance and same-sex marriage are being won in country and after country aided and assisted by the US State Department and the help of that Clinton woman. The battle is almost over. When Proposition 8 is finally overturned in California, traditional marriage will slowly die in America. Best of all, when state policy dictates that there are no differences between marriage and same-sex relationships, those individuals and organizations who oppose it become enemies of state policy, and state power will be brought to bear to make their consciences bend.

That is precisely what we want, Teufel - the total annihilation of orthodoxy of faith and morals. The cults and mega churches with their understanding of the faith is now so wishy-washy that it is barely distinguishable from the culture and Unitarianism, Biblical faith is an inch deep, and the state will rule with a rod of iron over opponents to the cultural zeitgeist.

We already have seen this dynamic at work in Massachusetts and the District of Columbia, where Catholic Charities was driven out of the adoption business because it prefers to place children with man-woman married couples. Judge Walker's decision on Proposition 8 has escalated the culture wars by officially labeling traditional religious believers and bodies as enemies of the core constitutional value of "equal protection."

A stroke of genius on your part, Teufel. Now is the time to drive home the wedges that divide (while continuing talk of dialogue of course) and keep in mind that our father is watching. The numbers that daily fill our devilish mansions tell the story. Keep the unfaith, Teufel, we are almost there and soon those true believers will have to lay down their lives for what they believe. It will be a sight to behold.

I remain your affectionate uncle,

Faust

ROWAN WILLIAMS SHADOWBOXING

My Dear Teufel,

The Anglican Communion is slowly but surely coming unglued while Dr. Rowan Williams' shadowboxes, placing form over substance. While this is sweet music to our ears, it is not playing out as we had hoped or anticipated.

The Global South archbishops and bishops are not buying his soft shoe approach to doctrine (Williams' private views on sodomy should not be confused with his public stance). They are beginning to see through him. While they are endlessly polite, their patience is running out. That must not be allowed to continue, Teufel. Nip it in the bud. Keep everybody at the table. Make sure Williams keeps singing the song of unity at all and any cost.

We were particularly concerned about Archbishop Henry Orombi's blunt statement that "diplomacy is dead" uttered recently in Uganda. Those are not words we want to hear. They highlight differences and negate all that talk made famous by Mrs. Jefferts Schori about the "other", a term that refers to anyone who no longer perceives themselves as White, Anglo-Saxon and vaguely Protestant. The guilt-ridden angst of effete white liberals bemoaning the plight of the "other" must continue to play itself out until it has run its course.

All that talk of the "other" plays up alleged white superiority and downplays, indeed downgrades, all talk of the need for the "other" to know the salvific work of Him whom we despise and long to destroy.

Of course, we knew all along that the acceptance of women's ordination would lead to the acceptance of sodomy, which in turn has led to litigation over properties. Once the flood gates of theological innovation were opened, we knew everything would finally tumble over the dam and into our father's many "mansions". It has all gone our way. Our father has been known to experience something close to joy.

As THE faith has all but evaporated in The Episcopal Church and in the Anglican Church of Canada, it behooves you to finish it off in the Church of England (including Scotland, Wales and Ireland), notwithstanding the Pope's recent visit to England. The recent spiritual bump by the Pope in England will soon evaporate amidst the growing gloom of secularism. You must begin to move more vigorously against the Global South.

Meantime continue to undermine the Anglo-Catholics by focusing on form and not the substance of the faith. Keep them focused on smells, bells and preferment. On the other hand, keep evangelicals alive with happy clappy theology and praise choruses. The key is to undermine, and if that fails, create a shadow of the reality as to what they believe. The most important thing is to keep the substance of the faith out of the pews and have pastors focus on MDG's, illegal immigration, and the need for more poofters in the pulpits.

Keep the lure of a purple shirt hanging over wannabe bishops. Power is such an aphrodisiac; it makes revisionists out of liberals, and liberals out of conservatives. The herd mentality must be maintained at all costs.

Once a priest hints that sex between a man and a woman in holy matrimony might be up for discussion, he is ours. Anyone who wavers just the tiniest bit on same sex unions, hinting that "faithfulness" in such unions might be the moral equivalent of heterosexual unions is on the road to perdition. He or she is ours.

Our Islamic brothers and sisters will aid you enormously in this task. Their pathological hatred of sodomy, Christians, Jews and Israel must continue to simmer and foment, with your help of course. Outbreaks of violence and intimidation serve us well, even as the simpering remains of liberal Christianity are being flushed down the Thames River aided and abetted by the likes of Jeffrey John, and Rowan Williams along with assorted liberal bishops, benign academics, priests in Holy Orders who believe little or nothing along with moderate men of all shades of opinion.

Keep the substance of the faith firmly away from the center of their thinking. Let them talk endlessly about the meaning of the resurrection, but make sure they never talk about the power of the risen Christ.

We have noticed that bishops who wear large crosses believe less about the atonement than those who don't. Form must always be made to triumph over substance, Teufel.

Make sure that words like "inclusion" and "diversity" are never far from their lips. Frank Griswold's "pluriform truths" has long since disappeared, but Jefferts Schori is inventing a whole new nomenclature to take TEC into the 21st century. The "other" and "conformity" as well as litigation are never far from her lips.

The anguished cries of the faux pain that liberals feel about anyone whose plight is less than their own must continue to resound throughout the land. We especially like hearing about "social justice" from bishops like Don Mathes of San Diego who lives in the ultra tony section of Kensington while sending his kids to private schools so they won't get contaminated by the "other." Such sweet music.

Let the liberals and revisionists rail against narrow-minded "fundamentalists" and the orthodox betrayal of the new world order of sexual diversity. The remaining orthodox must be made to feel guilty for not keeping up with the new-fangled "theology" of Vickie Gene Robinson, Jefferts Schori and TEC.

Now we were not happy to hear that that fellow Dan Martins has won the see of Springfield. He was clearly the most orthodox of the candidates and the most dangerous to our side. Make sure he does not receive consents. Work vigorously on the HOB and Diocesan Standing Committees. Start whispering campaigns that he is secretly homophobic...it will catch on with the liberal blogs and, like a brush fire, it will be all over the Internet. He will be toast. If he should obtain consents, make his life a living hell when he hits the ground running among the liberals. Make him regret he ever ran for the job.

In the meantime, declaw any good will or good feelings that may have remained with the recent visit of the Pope to England. He silenced the liberal press and his mea culpa over priestly abuse won him much respect, causing our father to vomit long into the night. We suspect, however, that the Pope may have touched many hearts with his plea for forgiveness.

What had our father positively enraged was the Pope's call for England to once again hear the claims of Christ and His uniqueness. Our father was apoplectic with rage when he heard this. His junior devils fled from his sight in abject fear when HIS name was mentioned.

Finally. We have just received word that a revolt has begun in the Diocese of South Carolina. The liberals in the diocese are rising up against Bishop Mark Lawrence. Excellent news. Foment this into a brush fire and then a full conflagration, Teufel.

In time, Bonnie Anderson and Jefferts Schori will be "forced" to intervene. They will move to expel Lawrence using some canon or other. Expect another Bonfire of the Inanities. TEC's bishops will move to get rid of Lawrence as they did Bob Duncan. The irony that they could not get rid of Charles Bennison brought our father out of his slump over the Pope's visit to England. This is the kind of ecclesiastical schizophrenia our father revels in. Keep up the good work.

I remain your affectionate uncle,

Faust

THE QUEEREST CHURCH ON EARTH

My dear Teufel,

What a thoroughly splendid year it has been for us. The Council of Hades met last week. Your name came up as one who has singularly honored us with your ability to undermine, prevaricate, destroy, deceive and provide the necessary waffle and fudge that has kept the Anglican Communion going.

You should take pride in your achievements, Teufel. A goblet of Pike's blood was passed around the council table in remembrance of you.

You have brought clarity where there was only guessing and wonderment. You have made The Episcopal Church the Queerest Church on earth (as it won't be in heaven). This achievement by itself will probably guarantee you a place at the council table within a decade or so. Like earthly law firms, you must first do the time before the elevation comes, but I can assure you that unless there is an outbreak of orthodoxy or one of those horrible spiritual revivals that occurs every so often when vulgar displays of public repentance and humility take place, then your place is assured at the council table. Well done.

The Glasspool election this past year was truly the icing on the fruit cake. Once again, The Episcopal Church stuck it in the face of Rowan Williams. He could only whimper that this would further strain relations within the communion. He wants The Episcopal Church to take a lesser role in the Anglican Communion. That will only happen when Hell freezes over and you know that won't happen. Of course, they just keep laughing at him, or conversely get angry with him for not casting his lot totally with the church's sodomites. Keep Colin Coward, Susan Russell and Louie Crew raging against the light. Their dark hearts are ours, all ours.

Our Father dragged up Hegel to dinner just to thank him. His whole thesis, antitheses, synthesis thing has worked well for us. Being neither hot nor cold but straddling the fence has worked well for us. Make sure the fence gets new more comfortable saddles for the spring, Teufel.

Also keep liberal bishops and archbishops preaching tolerance and beating up on Christians over so-called moderate Islamic mullahs and Imams. Nothing is sweeter music to our ears than watching Christians being persecuted and killed by Imams and their mob followers while watching liberal Anglican archbishops blast Christians for their alleged Islamophobia.

The one fly in the ointment that has our Father worried is the distancing of the Global South Primates from the more liberal and enlightened Primates.

That 11 archbishops will be no shows in Dublin is not something we relish at all. It will void Williams' ability to negotiate the nonnegotiable.

We loved it when he ran from room to room muttering "a pox on both your houses", but he loved the whole game. That is all it was. The poor fool and those on his left flank who believe that G-d has changed his mind about sexual behavior have pushed millions into our camp. It has been a stunning reversal of 2,000 years of church teaching.

We especially love all the eulogies to those who have died of HIV/AIDS, this year, especially the one in Vancouver, BC, Canada, recently that likened the death of Peter Jepson to John the Baptist by an Anglican archdeacon. That one had our Father in stitches...the howls could be heard all over Hades. http://www.vancouver.anglican.ca/portals/0/repository/Markusdrpetersermon.pdf

Make sure that public scorn is continually poured out on those who believe in reparative therapies. Have the cries of homophobia shouted from the roof tops. Under no circumstances must those who believe that same-sex attractions can be corrected be allowed any place in post-Christian North America and especially in a post-Christian Episcopal Church.

Keep the "Listening Process" alive as pushed by the liberals, revisionists and the ABC. We want the orthodox to have it shoved in their faces till they fall over in boredom or acceptance...(the latter is to our liking). You must remember that this is about desensitizing the orthodox so they just roll over. Listening is not about listening, but is about acquiescing to our side, Teufel. Keep the pressure and the checks rolling in. UNDER NO CIRCUMSTANCES are you to give any ground to the other side. They must be force fed and destroyed if necessary.

That Duncan fellow dropped a bomb shell at that horrible Lausanne Congress on Evangelism in Cape Town, South Africa, recently, when he said that Jefferts Schori and her ilk were out to exterminate the orthodox in TEC. He was right, of course, but what a horrible revelation. We can't touch him. Unfortunately, a great cloud of witnesses and angels surrounds him. Our Father grinds his teeth every time his name is mentioned.

The trip switch for 2011, Teufel, will be the destruction of the Diocese of South Carolina and its bishop, Mark Lawrence. With the new canons giving more power to the national church than the sovereign rights of local dioceses, see that David Booth Beers is geared up to wreak havoc on this diocese.

Keep the pansexual mill alive in 2011, Teufel. We noted with interest that the road to legalizing same-sex marriage has led to the floodgates opening. Any and all forms of sexuality are now fair game for legalization and promotion.

Homosexual marriage was simply the thin edge of the wedge. Our full-frontal assault on the institutions of marriage and family means there is no logical reason to prevent other deviant types of sexuality from being recognized and legitimized.

So, it was absolutely wonderful news to read recently that there is now a push to legalize incest.

The slippery slope, which was ridiculed and mocked by some on our side claiming no one is arguing for polyamory or incest, is now coming to pass. There are people all over the world pushing for these very things. They are happy to ride on the success of the same-sex marriage movement, much to our delight.

We noted with gladness that the upper house of the Swiss parliament has drafted a law decriminalizing sex between consenting family members which must now be considered by the government. There have been only three cases of incest since 1984. No matter, Teufel, once it is legislated in, there will be no holding back the floodgates.

The final sexual barriers are coming down across the world, Teufel. We must make sure that churches, especially the Episcopal Church and the Anglican Church of Canada, which once followed the culture, will now be in the vanguard for total change. It is a triumph that only our Father could have dreamed of. Now it will be yours to implement.

I remain your affectionate uncle,

Faust

21ST CENTURY SEXUAL DIVERSITY

My dear Teufel,

The Council of Hades met recently and concluded with a toast to your splendid services for your ongoing magnificent efforts in steering the Episcopal Church so firmly in our direction. A pint of Bishop Pike's blood was drunk in your honor.

We have not seen its like since the formation of the National Council of Churches and all the smoke blown in peoples' faces about ecumenicity and, now, all the recent talk of interfaith alliances. It is all such sweet music to our ears. The more befuddlement, the better. The mush god of interfaith talk must be promoted and extended far and wide, just like the call for pansexual acceptance in the name of justice. On no account must faith be personalized and homosexual behavior and its consequences talked about.

We especially like the nice linguistic turns of phrases so prevalent in discourses on pansexuality by various Episcopal bishops.

"We must engage in more than a monologue by having a 21st century conversation on sexual diversity, with new and different voices heard from." Ah, what sweet music to our ears, Teufel.

"This [series] will show the variety of viewpoints on issues of sexual diversity among Episcopalians. Each event has a unique focus, and, as a whole, they will lift up new voices that are rarely heard and raise awareness about the impact of church teachings and public stances of the lives of LGBT people."

We especially like this line. "The goal is to encourage more vigorous, honest, and open debate about sexual diversity within and outside the Episcopal Church."

Of course we know that this is a flat out lie. The goal is not to encourage more debate ... that is modernist code and disingenuous double speak for throwing Church teaching overboard and continuing the revolution of evil that has swamped the Church in the west for half a century ... and counting. It is, of course, precisely what we want you to encourage.

So it is very important, my dear Teufel, to regularly update the language to make it sound more, shall we say, inclusive and heart-warming...it certainly warms our Father's heart to see more and more folk drop into our camp. The little bishop of Iowa, Walter Righter fell into our Father's House this past week swelling the ranks of Episcopal bishops. Have no fear, we have plenty of spaces for more heretical bishops. Our Father awaits their coming.

That Ragsdale woman who heads the Episcopal Divinity School said, "Abortion is a Blessing...and our work is not done". What a gem. If only we could clone her and put her in every seminary in America. That she is also President and Executive Director of something called Political Research Associates, which describes itself as "a progressive think tank devoted to supporting movements that are building a more just and inclusive democratic society," is such sweet music to our ears, Teufel. Under no circumstances must doctrine or Scripture enter into any sort of dialogue when talk of inclusivity is raised. Inclusion must exclude any talk of moral absolutes. Keep them talking about "spirituality" not the Holy Spirit.

Promoting sodomy in the name of academic freedom is a mantra worth repeating. Phrases like "generous orthodoxy" or "generous pastoral response" are sweet music to our Father's ears.

The Listening Process, which everyone knows has nothing to do with listening at all, must be continued if just to blow fog in the faces of those damnable orthodox Global South bishops. It is all a subterfuge to broker in pansexuality and dumb down Global South bishops into thinking their point of view is being honored and respected. We know, of course, that it is not so, it must be maintained at all costs, even when Rowan departs Lambeth Palace - a huge loss I might point out. His waffling and prevarications on moral issues along with his near total inability to articulate a faith anybody could remotely understand got agent Slubnose a special commendation from Our Father.

The broader cultural wars talk of "chastity" and "virginity" must be expunged or, at the very least, diluted in the name of being "pastoral". "Pastoral" should be translated as concerned, caring, and, above all, non-judgmental. People must be true to themselves, whatever that means and wherever it may lead. Under no circumstances must they bow the knee to Him. Man must be the measure of all things and the highest authority. Being "pastoral" undermines the very salvation we want them to avoid. We know that "pastoral" is a code word for cowardice and, in some cases, agreement. Fill the universities and seminaries with men and women who are pastoral types, simpering milquetoast, weak, spineless, ineffectual and bland persons of all shades of opinion; pastors who can't wait to fall all over themselves being pastoral to all who knock on their door. Being "pastoral" threatens to seriously undermine the very salvation of those in their care.

This continual furtherance of the homosexual agenda in The Episcopal Church must be pushed to new and higher levels of full inclusion of ALL sexualities. If you can include the S & M bondage crowd, cross dressers and all manner of decadent types, by all means, do so. The church must be made to feel their pain of exclusion. Keep Episcopal bishops riding in open Cadillacs at gay pride parade days waving to crowds so they can be seen for how wonderfully inclusive and open and caring they are. What poor fools and dupes they have become Teufel. Every time there is a gay parade of one sort or another, our Father holds a feast in anticipation of their coming. We particularly like this from the Diocese of Atlanta. "Integrity Atlanta maintains an open and welcoming atmosphere encouraging the participation in the service of all people whether female or male, straight or gay, lesbian, bisexual, transgendered, questioning, African American, Hispanic, Latino, white, black, brown -- the entire rainbow of God's created humanity."

What we especially like is that there is absolutely no protection of children. These fools, including the Bishop of Atlanta, expose the "least of these" - vulnerable children - to this wholesale perversion. How positively delicious, Teufel. Keep it up.

Your seduction of the innocent is working brilliantly. The oppression of those who must have an abortion, regardless of the spiritual, eternal, emotional and personal cost, must be buried beneath a woman's right to do exactly as she pleases with her body regardless of personal and societal consequences. A woman must be made to feel liberated even if her immortal soul is endangered. We must never let people know that sexual liberation can lead to soul damnation.

Continue to turn up the heat by revisionist Episcopal bishops on the dwindling orthodox in the name of inclusion. The oppression of the oppressed must be sustained at all costs. Keep the property wars going; deplete their financial resources till their coffers run dry on both sides. We win either way.

Keep the magenta crowd (bishops) more focused on the weight of the cross around their necks than on the weightier meaning of the cross for their salvation. Of course, we know that most TEC bishops have rejected the true meaning of the cross these days, which was the brilliant work of one of your predecessors. Liberal theology, Gay Theology, Interfaith alliances, and Liberation theology is all a continuum, Teufel, that leads straight to hell and to Our Father. The Episcopal bishops, led by that Presiding Bishop woman, meeting in Ecuador this week have resurrected the dead dog of Liberation Theology. I doubt we could have made this stuff up. Our Father was in danger of busting a gut when he heard the news.

Keep up the good work, Teufel. Never miss an opportunity to twist, prevaricate, slice and dice, shuffle and pervert their wretched gospel at every opportunity...

I remain your affectionate uncle,

Faust

THE CODE OF OMERTA

My dear Teufel,

The news is quite alarming. We hear that this Jefferts Schori woman deliberately received a known pederast priest into the Episcopal Church when she was Bishop of Nevada and now she has been found out. This could prove disastrous to our side and the cause she and we believe in. We insist that you move all hell (if you'll pardon the pun) to ensure she is not charged or brought to trial for her actions. It would be a huge loss to our side if this was to happen and she was tossed out of The Episcopal Church.

Make sure the House of Bishops is duly cowed into silence "the silence of the Episcopal lambkins". If anyone has the stomach to rise up and charge her based on the new canons, which were pushed and promoted by her, it would be disastrous. Make sure that all the dark and dirty secrets of bishops that Bethlehem Bishop Paul Marshall hinted at are used to keep them quiet and acquiescent. Make sure that Bishop Clayton Matthews, Jefferts Schori's Consigliere for bad boy bishops who knows all the secrets, kicks into high gear. The code of omerta must be in play. See that someone sends him a new pair of thumbscrews for anyone who gets out of line.

We need her, Teufel. She is doing marvelous work undermining their precious gospel. Now that she is exporting the Episcopal Church's Culture Wars into Africa, she is needed now, more than ever. We could not have created her. Her recent denial of the Incarnation was sweet music to our ears.

It would appear that the newly installed Bishop of Washington Mariann Budde is giving the New Age movement a push right into the heart of TEC. A budding Aquarian if ever there was one. I see the future of the cathedral Teufel with anti-Christian movements such as Focusing: Doorway to the body-life of spirit, Reiki training, Eco-Spirituality, Star in My Heart with Sophia and She is God, Reflexology, Praying with Kabir, Centering Prayer, The Enneagram, Dancing with the Cosmos, Creation-Centered Spirituality using Matthew Fox's work. If they haven't already openly denied the deity of Him they soon will. The crushing determination of our father will have them all in our camp. Hell awaits.

That those foolish evangelical Africans allowed a communications unit into the CAPA offices in Nairobi was a major coup for our side. The ACC types in London and TEC in New York and Integrity in Calipornia will use it to push the West's pansexual Anglican agenda and "Listening Process" right down their throats at every opportunity with stories of aggrieved homosexuals and lesbians. Oh the pain!

Keep the pressure on the bishop of South Carolina. The most important thing is dissension within the ranks. We hear there are three groups forming now. There are, of course, the Forum dissenters who believe in the Episcopal Church come hell or high water. Then there is the bulk of the diocese that will follow Mark Lawrence whatever he and they decide. (We hear that it is to the Middle East and Bishop Mouneer.) Then there is a third group ready to blow the diocese and perhaps link up with the ACNA or some other Anglican jurisdiction. Anything you can do to divide is to our liking but be aware that the conservative blogs are making hay out of the fact that while Jefferts Schori goes after Lawrence on the newly minted Title IV canons, she herself could face charges. Go lightly, Teufel, but carry a big stick.

The most important thing is to keep the masquerade of orthodoxy alive. Phrases like "generous orthodoxy" maintain the illusion; linguistic conjuror's tricks are our specialty.

The recent interview given by former PB Frank Griswold that TEC and the other mainline denominations are going through a "desert time" was such sweet music to our father's ears, that he drank a newly corked pint of Bishop Walter Righter's blood. The cackles of glee could be heard all over hell. These poor fools have no idea what they are saying and doing, the damage they are doing or where it is all heading! It's as if they have blinders on to the hell they have created on earth and the ultimate hell they will fall into after they have died.

That they believe that they can actually overturn the moral order and survive has been their downfall. Their blindness in the face of continued church losses, at times, boggles our father's mind, and let me tell you that that is hard to do. Stalin, Hitler, Il Duce, Marx, Engels, Freud and Ayn Rand were easy targets, especially Freud, Marx and Rand who were Jews. When Jews lose their religion, they become the worst tyrants, Teufel. Upend the intelligentsia and the crowds will follow like sheep. Money, sex and power remain our best weapons, but the subversion of the Faith is our primary objective. You must be as cunning as The Serpent in the Garden who, of course, taught us everything.

It was Marx who overturned the political order and brought the Soviet Union to a standstill for 72 years. More than 60 million people were killed under Joseph Stalin. Freud, the father of sexual liberation, was dubbed by our father as the "godfather of AIDS", a real treasure I might add. Ayn Rand, the high priestess of economic Darwinism, made a god of greed that brought about the collapse of the markets in 2008 with disciples like Alan Greenspan aiding and abetting her philosophy.

Of course, this did have the adverse effect of many turning back to Him in their hours of anguish and loss, but the damage done to greed was only temporary.

It is the religious types, specifically Christians that we want subverted and their foul doctrines overturned. That is our biggest challenge and foremost objective, Teufel. Couple that subversion with the rise of Islam and we will see the decline of the West continue in helter-skelter fashion.

Progressing from ecumenicity to interfaith alliances has been a short step in a continued downward spiral.

What you must seek to do is to neutralize the claims of Him by talk of equality among all religions. His uniqueness is what undermines us. Here is where your unique skills come in, Teufel.

Draw religious leaders together in gabfests around the world. Let all the leaders come in their various robes and look the part. Let them bow and scrape to one another and give papers on peace, love and justice, but under no circumstances must talk of Him be mentioned. If His name comes up, neutralize it by talk of Him being the friend of all with discrimination for none. Let him be named as a Great Teacher, a humble servant, a great philosopher, a lover of all mankind but under no circumstances must words like atonement and "peace with God through Him" and expressions like "being washed clean in the blood of the Lamb" come from their throats. That is the language of exclusivity and it must be avoided at all costs. Images of the cross, which we have effectively neutralized in movies and with muscle-bound idiots and teenagers, who have them tattooed into their skin, are now a caricature. It's the serious Christian players that you must undermine…those evangelicals and Catholics who still take their religion seriously. They must be undermined at all costs. One of the most advantageous moves is to keep them arguing among themselves; it deflects them from their real mission. The Ordinariate is just a side show.

When the Pope went to Germany and Austria, recently, and began his pilgrimage with a talk to Lutherans, our father was apoplectic with rage. That is NOT the kind of thing we want to see happen. That IS the kind of ecumenicity our father and the council of Hades find threatening. If the orthodox of all Christian denominations start talking seriously about what holds them together "namely the faith itself -- we are doomed, Teufel.

We read with horror what that wretched Duncan fellow said in Pittsburgh recently. He revealed that Anglican congregations are in partnership with Methodist congregations, Presbyterian congregations, Non-denominational congregations, and Catholic congregations for new homes and meeting places, and even some shared ministries. "We meet here in this Benedictine Abbey and College as a sign of what has happened. God has provided new friends and encouragers for our post-exodus journey. We are much more - yet possessing much less - than we were before."

This is our worst nightmare, Teufel. Liberalism and revisionism are forcing alliances on the other side that we could not have envisaged and it is deeply troubling to the Council of Hades who met in special conclave recently to consider the matter. We may have to put more demons onto the situation.

Mind how you go, Teufel. Our father is not above punishing even his best agents for failure and, truly, you do not want to cross him.

I remain your affectionate uncle,

Faust

THE GLORIOUS DAMAGE OF KATHARINE JEFFERTS-SCHORI

My dear Teufel,

It is hard not to imagine the enormous damage this Jefferts Schori woman is doing to her church and faith. I doubt we could have come up with someone like her - a woman who spent most of her early life examining squid and then does a 180-degree turn and examines Scripture with the clinical detachment of a plate of fried calamari. Our Father says she will be given first class accommodations when she arrives here, at least for a while, but never enough ease for the torment that will follow.

She has undermined their wretched faith and the weak-willed House of Bishops who follows her like lemmings over a cliff. They are simply unaware (or refuse to see) that she has given the whole shop away....to us. There is always the concern, though we admit rather limited, that the penny might suddenly drop as the church slowly empties and she as Presiding Bishop declare a "national state of calamity". With your help this will not happen.

It never ceases to amaze us, Teufel. In the old days, we had to work hard for converts. Newer atheists like Richard Dawkins, Christopher Hitchens, and Sam Harris (to name perhaps the three most famous examples) proudly proclaim from whatever atheistic minaret they can find that the idea of God is a delusion, that the God of the Bible is not great, and that "faith" should be, are our best advertisers. They were difficult converts, but once seduced, they became some of our best agent provocateurs. They are, of course, the heirs of such minds as A. J. Ayer, H.G. Wells and the Bloomsbury set. Wells' book Mind at the End of its Tether almost gave the whole game away. Mercifully the book never went viral.

But Jefferts Schori is a dream come true and beyond anything we could have hoped for. Pansexual knock off sinners like Otis Charles, Mary Glasspool, Gene Robinson, Louie Crew, Susan Russell, Tracey Lind et al were easy prey and third-rate sinners at that. Just twist an already twisted culture on sex a little further and, presto, the church was sure to follow. From pop goes the weasel to pop goes the condom was a short sexual highway.

The morals of The Episcopal Church now lie somewhere between Two and a Half Men and The Big Bang Theory. Why they haven't offered the lesbian talk show host Ellen DeGeneres a deanship or something is quite beyond us. I suppose Tracey Lind will have to do. It was unfortunate Lind did not become the next bishop of New York; we could have made her an instant celebrity. We could have had her and Frank Griswold do the Circle Dance of Dispossession together on U-Tube for all the world to see.

I must tell you, Teufel, that the Presiding Bishop's latest pronouncements have been making the rounds in Hades with considerable mirth and entertainment.

This Sarah Frances Ives woman catches the flavor of her thinking. "In Jefferts Schori's recent book, The Heartbeat of God, she cleverly weaves together her vision of the future Episcopal Church-interfaith communities partnered with a huge United States government. She writes, it is all about, 'Mission, mission, mission', (91) and describes many different projects that parishes can start in tandem with the government and other secular groups. Jefferts Schori's underlying terror in this book is clear: create more projects at the parishes or the Episcopal Church is going to disappear. Get to work, peons. Our ship is sinking.

"She tells us what to do about any problem in glib and superficial terms that include disparate advice such as to eat our protein, wash our dishes by hand, celebrate layoffs in the Episcopal Church, support the Obama health care bill, call ourselves beloved, criticize the Archbishop of Canterbury Rowan Williams, make the United States government limit capitalistic profits, declare unity in the Episcopal Church, and plant gardens on the church lawns.

"Jefferts Schori bounces from one subject to another with the rapidity of a writer not disciplined by transitional ideas or even rational thought. On page 23 within four sentences, Jefferts Schori drags in, with her typical pell-mell fashion, Katrina and its aftermath, genocide in Rwanda, global AIDS, torture for terrorists, and health care reform in our country. With all her vast pronouncements, she doesn't even bother with a bibliography to support her ideas and includes only seven notes for quotes (two of which are from the Book of Common Prayer)."

This is precisely the kind of glib educated intelligentsia of the 21st Century that we seek, Teufel, -- smart one-liners with little or no substance. The sheer hypocrisy of the TEC House of Bishops meeting recently in Quito, Ecuador, bemoaning global warning while increasing their own carbon footprints had us all in hysterical fits.

Keep the Episcopal deep thinkers and their followers focusing on this world with all its joys and pain, but never, I repeat never, must they be allowed to think of the life to come with its unspeakable joy for those who follow Him and the torment that awaits those who reject their vile faith here.

Allow them to luxuriate in blasting ordinary Christians as uneducated "fundamentalists", unscientific fools unable to tell the difference between a limpet and a limpet mine, but never must the enormity of their lost salvation be on their mental radar screen. John Shelby Spong is a genius working for us at this level.

Make them feel secure in their lostness. Make them believe that there is nothing out there; that it all ends in death and nothingness. Any notions of eternal life and light or eternal death and darkness must be expunged from their minds. Let them believe that this world IS all there is, that they must live it to its fullest while grabbing the gold ring. Make sure that Ayn Rand's books do the rounds. Her gospel of greed has made the US a selfish, greedy nation. It MUST be everybody's gospel, not just Wall Street brokers and Federal Reserve chairmen. Love of self without love of neighbor must be paramount. American minds are dull with endless hours of television, porno and the good life. Make sure that the part about the "pursuit of happiness" is never far from their minds. To parody, "For me to live is gain and to die is no loss at all."

That Jefferts Schori has actually twisted their gospel into this worldly salvation is but the end game of 50 years of Protestant liberalism and their "social gospel", just as AIDS is the climax, if you'll pardon the pun, of the 60's sexual revolution. Sigmund Freud has served our Father well as the high priest of sexual liberation. Intellectual Jewish elites who have abandoned the Torah are our best allies and twisters of truth.

As we are in the season of HIS incarnation make sure people can be heard to say Happy Holidays and not Merry Christmas, make sure the ACLU sues anyone who tries to fill the public square with Christian symbols like creches...anything to remind them of what the birth of HIM really means. If the masses ever catch on, it would be over for us. You must never let that happen Teufel.

We relish the growing secularization of America. It is sweet music to our ears when, day by day, people are caught up in the Culture of Celebrity sacrificing their souls for momentary pleasures and passing toys, substituting the real thing for fantasy.

The pressure you must exert in 2012 is increasing secularization, the dumbing down of Christian absolutes, more talk of interfaith alliances, the neutering of doctrine, the increasing legitimization of gay marriage, gay rites and all manner of things pansexual. Any opposition must be met with cries of homophobia and lawsuits designed to put the fear of Hades into them. Make the Bible look stupid or like just one more holy book among many. Keep all talk of exclusive claims of HIM at bay. Dumb HIM down as a mere prophet, one among many, a good man, one to follow in doing good things, a super Mother Teresa, but never as Lord and Savior or true Master of the Universe. THAT must be repelled at all costs.

The Council of Hades met recently and much admired your work in 2011. Our Father drank a pint of one resident Episcopal bishops' blood in your honor. A special medal is also being cast in your honor for the great achievements you accomplished this past year. They were astounding. Some jealous observations were expressed, which our Father reveled in. We ARE hoping for more and better results in 2012. These are dark days and the darker the better. Mind how you go with the persecution of Christians in Nigeria and the Middle East, Teufel. These things can backfire on us, the blood of the martyrs being the seed of the church and all that.

Nonetheless I remain your affectionate uncle,

Faust

DELEGATED EPISCOPAL PASTORAL OVERSIGHT TURNED ON ITS HEAD

My dear Teufel,

What an absolute stroke of genius. You managed to turn that DEPO business on its head and use it to our benefit. Totally brilliant, my dear Teufel. Orthodox Episcopalians had hoped that they could use Delegated Episcopal Pastoral Oversight to get out from under liberal and revisionist bishops. You have turned it round making it possible for liberal priests and parishes in the Diocese of Albany to get out from under that dreadful Love fellow and his evangelical catholic orthodoxy and freely join an arch-liberal bishop like Gladstone Adams, without doubt one of the worst in The Episcopal Church and a bishop much to our liking.

He once gave a pass to a pedophile priest who later got caught and jailed. He then gave himself a pass for covering it up and managed to destroy an orthodox Episcopal priest in the process. This man is totally with us. You need to encourage more like him. Keep infiltrating the remaining handful of orthodox dioceses and undermine them. We think you should turn your considerable skills on the Diocese of

South Carolina. See if you can wreck more havoc there. To date, Bishop Mark Lawrence has managed to stick it to Presiding Bishop Jefferts Schori keeping her hands-off properties as well as Lawrence. It is very important that you whip her into a frenzy about this, once again, and make her feel unloved and rejected. You could even foment some discord among the Forum crowd.

It seems that Mrs. Jefferts Schori has outed herself quite openly by abandoning traditional sexual morality and dumping Jewish law (which she misinterprets). Excellent. Instead, she wants a new world order where traditional Christian understandings of morality are abandoned. This is such sweet music to our ears, Teufel.

This pseudo morality of hers must be played up and disseminated as widely as possible. The Africans won't buy it, but there are some decidedly weak Anglican links in Asia and Latin America that she can exploit and we along with her.

Sex is such a malleable and pliable behavior and so self-justifying. The Council of Hades drank a toast to her continuing push for immorality and making it acceptable to the masses, especially to Episcopalians. That she writes this with an eye to justifying the current situation by destroying traditional understandings of sexuality found in the Hebrew law and giving favor to TEC's acceptance of post-modern sexual norms is precisely the kind of undermining of the church's very moral foundations that we want her to embrace and promulgate.

We notice that her train of thought is seeping quite nicely into all the mainline Protestant denominations. Add a little pop psychology, "me too" triumphalism, (a speech or two from Gene Robinson whining about the need for homosexual acceptance) some "feel your pain" emotionalism, a dose of victimhood add a little neutered theology to the mix and, hey, presto, we have them all in the bag.

We especially like that line in her book "God is at work in all this 'inappropriate sexual behavior.'" I doubt our father could have come up with a better line. He was actually heard chortling so loudly when he read this that many feared he had lost his mind. Fortunately, that's not possible. His deviant mind grows better with time.

Jefferts Schori calls prostitution a creative survival. Her motto seems to be "Do what it takes," and don't judge with critical and simplistic standards, i.e. the Jewish law. In making such pronouncements, she has dismissed the entire Christian heritage as well as the Jewish law and the prophets. This is stunning Teufel, you need to make sure the other mainline denominations buy this hook, line and sinker. Add the word "fundamentalist" to anyone who believes in straitjacket thinking and the whole Western Protestant church is ours.

In time, she will dismiss the Ten Commandments as she has the much bally-hoed Covenant that she said is past its shelf life. Her theology creates a life void of hope and redemption that is much to be desired. MAKE sure such voids are filled with pleasure, endless hours of texting, e-mailing, iPodding, pornography and much more. Never allow a vacuum, Teufel. It is in moments like these that people start thinking and we certainly do not want that to happen. (We were alarmed to read that Richard Dawkins, in a debate with Rowan Williams, opened the possibility that God might exist and has moved from his outright atheism to agnosticism. This is terribly dangerous, Teufel. It is a short hop from there to theism and true belief. THAT would be a total disaster.)

This is precisely the kind of false hermeneutic that we like. At the end of the day, Jefferts Schori has undermined the very morality she has sworn to uphold. What we are observing is the nation's most prominent religious institutions and a number of its political leaders accompanying her in this.

We are now seeing moral relativity being carried over into the political sphere in spades. We have politicians screaming that they don't want government peering into the bedrooms of the nation, but support the government to fund contraceptive devices, birth control pills, free abortion, and drugs to fight HIV/AIDS without anyone daring to call into question the sexual behaviors that cause all this disease and death. That Santorum fellow is positively dangerous. Get those politicians back on track talking money, jobs and the economy. We don't want them to think they are being endangered by practices that can destroy their very souls.

Make sure Jefferts Schori continues to tear down all boundaries and Biblical understandings of sexual morality that leads her church and all humanity into a nightmare of confusion and chaos. Her own church's endorsement of LGBTQI is increasingly destructive of traditional standards for sexual behavior. Under no circumstances must she actually SEE women and men involved in the sex industry and how it degrades women for men's pleasure. Let her feel liberated from all sexual restraints and keep further distancing herself and her church's real teachings from the liberation and redemption offered by Him.

On no account must she speak of a Savior who longs to redeem their lives. Blending together the identity of homosexual and lesbian priests with female priests is an added epistemological and moral stereotyping that should be exploited to the hilt.

The other thing we notice with much glee is that she is seeking to change the Episcopal Church into multi-faith centers practicing blended spiritualities. Teufel, you need to keep pushing the Washington National Cathedral as the locus of the new World Spiritual Order. That Washington Bishop Mariann Budde woman is hopelessly lost. Make sure she keeps wandering endlessly and hopelessly in the desert of her own labyrinth till her head falls off.

Above all, Teufel, keep alive the notion that God is infinitely tolerant and given to sudden changes of mind - a divinity that is endlessly pliable and will keep up with the multiple moral changes of Jefferts Schori and TEC's House of Bishops.

It was Victor Hugo who once famously said, "When God desires to destroy a thing, he entrusts its destruction to the thing itself. Every bad institution of this world ends by suicide."

The Episcopal Church's Presiding Bishop is heading with Gadarene speed toward the cliff's edge. See that she encounters no impediments, Teufel. We want them all to go down together.

I remain your affectionate uncle,

Faust

2012 YEAR IN REVIEW

My Dear Teufel,

2012. What a year. Once again Americans confused license with freedom and their Gadarene slide towards us continues at even greater speed. The president now says he believes in Gay marriage, with the whole LGBTQI agenda being pushed in every state and promoted in nearly all the major Protestant denominations is sweet music to our Father's ears. Make sure the gay Washington lobbies have pots of money to keep the political pressure on.

We note, with interest, the arrival here this past week of Bishop Jane Holmes Dixon of Washington, DC. What a piece of work she is. She did incredible damage to the orthodox cause in the Diocese of Washington following the venal reign of Ronald Haines who is also with us. (He never allowed one straight white male priest to find a parish in his diocese...only women and gays were welcome). Now that she is here, we are showing her the damage she wrought on our behalf. She spends most of her time in tears, unable to fathom how and why she is with us in Hell and not on the other side. We play the tapes of her life as a bishop right down to the ugly glares she gave humble servants of Him, the money spent on lawsuits, and her beating up of one lonely g-d-fearing priest. She is made to watch it on a repeated loop so it sinks in that she was always our servant and not the servant of Him. The revelations have knocked her for a loop. Our father quietly gloats as he anticipates the arrival of more Episcopal bishops in the months and years ahead.

But, on to business. We were shocked to learn that Rowan Williams' replacement is an evangelical cut from the ALPHA, Carey, and Coggan mold. This is a disastrous turn of events. That the Queen gave ol' Rowan a life peerage and that he will henceforth be known as Baron Williams of Oystermouth had our father in stitches. OYSTERMOUTH for Hell's sake. Our Father hates it when the British outdo themselves with their dark irony and sardonic humor. What a black pearl Williams turned out to be.

This Welby fellow, however, poses a serious threat to our final takeover and co-opting of Western Anglicanism. We almost had it in the bag with the Church of England. Endless talk of social justice, women bishops, and sodomy...it was all moving in our direction when then this geeky looking oil executive comes along and says he actually believes in HIM. Our Father was apoplectic and was heard to rage around hell, so much so that even his closest minions quivered and quaked for days. Now he has calmed down a bit and is working on a new strategy to undermine Welby. There are some here who are saying we overplayed our hand. If so, we must work harder to change that.

I see that Canadian archbishop fellow Hiltz came a calling and demanded that Welby not recognize Duncan and the ACNA. An excellent move, Teufel. Make sure Hiltz holds Welby's feet to the fire.

There must be no capitulation; we are almost there. And make sure Welby accepts another invitation from Jefferts Schori to meet with her House of Bishops. Those are defining moments. Clubbiness is what it is all about, not truth. Keep Welby FEELING good about these American bishops. Make sure he sips wine with Glasspool and Robinson over cheese and crackers. Make it caviar, if necessary. Under no circumstances must he be allowed to see or hear about TEC's dark side of dwindling parishes, plummeting incomes, and all the millions being spent on lawsuits for properties.

Let the HOB have meaningless discussions about homoousios and homoiousios. Let them chatter on about "of one substance" or "same essence." Just make sure they come back to the homo bit and the vacuous smiley face of Gene. That man can tip toe his way through a gay bathhouse wearing a rainbow miter while handing out condoms and Gay TEC Bibles with all the sincerity of a dog in heat.

Of course, our best recourse is the American presiding bishop herself. What an absolute gem she has turned out to be. She doesn't even pretend to believe in the deity of Him or his bodily resurrection. Even our Father below believes in that and trembles. I doubt we could have created a facsimile of a woman like her. Use her, Teufel, as she is our best and perhaps last resort in undermining the whole of Western Anglicanism with all her sublime talk of Millennium Development Goals and the Five Marks of Mission. Under no circumstances must she talk about HIM as Lord and Savior or sin and salvation. Such words (easily found on the lips of Welby) must immediately be squashed.

The irony was not lost on our Father when the Diocese of Pennsylvania, with the help of the National Church, managed to unload Bishop Charles E. Bennison. It turned out he was even too much for the Church liberals to keep on so they got rid of him. The liberals at GC2012 rammed through a canon that was able to get rid of one of their own...irony indeed. Bennison will be heartily welcomed when he arrives here. That he virtually destroyed the Anglo-Catholics in the diocese, cowed the evangelicals, and closed down more parishes than virtually any other bishop has made him a hero in our Father's eyes.

Now it is very important that you allow, yea, even encourage conservative groups like the Anglican Communion Institute and the Communion Partners to weep, wail, and gnash their collective teeth against The Episcopal Church and its leaders; they need a place to vent. But we both know they were neutered by our Father long ago and made powerless to effectively change anything. As long as they remain institutionalists, they belong to us. Tennessee Bishop John Bauerschmidt is a perfect example of roll over. He's a CP bishop we were told, but as soon as he was faced with a church - St. Andrews, Nashville - leaving TEC, he behaved like Attila the Hun. He acted as his New York ecclesiastical mistress expected and sued and won the property. He then said there are no plans to hold Sunday services there. Make sure it is sold to an Islamic group, Teufel. Shove it in their faces. Our Father laughs at their pathetic compromises. It never ceases to awe him how easy it is for them to roll over.

They are so far from NT Christianity it amazes Him and the High Council. We give constant praise to our Father who makes sure they never go to Nigeria or Uganda to see what authentic Christianity really looks like as they might be shamed into acting and believing differently. Make sure the Boko Haram keep killing Christians in Northern Nigeria. TEC bishops won't go near the place. They have nothing to die for and they certainly wouldn't lay down their lives for their Anglican brothers.

Make sure they never compromise, Teufel. Make sure words like "generous orthodoxy", inclusivity, and diversity are buzzwords embedded in their brains till death do them part. Make sure the constant whine of pansexualists yelling "justice" and "rights" is constantly in the forefront of liberal and moderate bishops thinking; morality be damned. Make sure the constant shrill cry of lesbians like [the Rev.] Susan Russell is heard in all their ears and they feel her pain. We don't want a repeat of South Carolina.

In the end, they will all be ours, Teufel. All ours.

Our Father hails your efforts Teufel, but we must never forget that the other side has huge resources at its disposal. Keep undermining them. Your reward and a senior place in our father's kingdom are assured. Retirement is out of the question.

I remain your affectionate uncle,

Faust

EPISCOPAL VICTIMS OF SOUTH CAROLINA

My dear Teufel,

So, the South Carolina Episcopalians have split with the minority playing the victim in the face of Bishop Mark Lawrence's venality and intransigence. Make sure the press plays up the "fundamentalism", "narrowness" and doctrinaire bishop and his fundie followers. Their lack of inclusion and diversity must ring around the communion and across the world. Paint them as the worst kind of narrow minded persons, never mind that "their way" is indeed narrow and "few there be that find it." You must paint Presiding Bishop Jefferts Schori and her crowd as the open-minded ones, open to change and the winds of the spirit, whatever the hell that is and wherever the hell they blow. They blow of course right into our father's furnace.

Keep the talk all sweetness and light, inviting those who did not cross the road with them to come back by warm invitation into the bosom of TEC...a bosom overflowing with largess and luminosity, but with fewer dollars. After all she is going to need several million dollars to finance lawsuits against Lawrence and his diocese, so one might have to contribute to that fund. Furthermore, remind them that they are still part of the Anglican Communion whereas Lawrence is not, and that HIS arms are wide enough to embrace all regardless of sexual orientation, even religion and not the stunted medieval dogma of those ghastly orthodox types.

At all times, religion must be conceived of in the broadest possible terms; that His love has no boundaries, all are embraced with no thought to behavior and discipleship (a horrible word) that forces people to conclude that it is "my will" and not "thy will" be done. Therein lies the harder, higher road and under no circumstances must that be taken.

The easy road leads to us, Teufel, so pave it with good intentions, half-hearted commitments, all sexualities, endless social projects and concerns for the "other". Let them chatter on about interfaith and interface, showing deep tearful concern for the "other" that they have no interest in converting. Under no circumstances must the fearful sight of a crucified Christ (I hate even to say the word) be visible on their spiritual radar screens. Divert, divert, divert. Keep people endlessly playing on their i-phones, i-Pads, chattering meaningless nonsense on Facebook and the half dozen social media that now inhabit the earth. Keep them endlessly tweeting, twittering and texting; but NEVER must they come to a knowledge of the truth that could radically change their lives and force them into a new direction. Keep the Kardashians not Christ ever before them.

The next move, and one I have positioned a personal demon onto, is that dreadful evangelical Archbishop-elect Justin Welby. We almost had it in the bag with Rowan of Oystermouth. Then the Church of England goes and does the darndest thing; they go for another George Carey type. This is too horrible to contemplate. Undermining him is now our top priority. The failure by Agent Slubnose to neutralize that ALPHA movement has caused our father great perplexity and deep pain that he will undoubtedly inflict on others, in due course.

Mercifully, The Episcopal Church is almost all ours with only a small handful of holdout dioceses. In time, they will elect moderates (we do so love them) as they think they are doing His will and not ours. Really nasty bishops like Spong, Righter, Dixon, Bruno, Jefferts Schori et al are too obvious. Obviously ours are the subtler ones, keep our serpentine father in a special hellish mode of artful glee as he contemplates their arrival with oh so much unctuousness. "Good day to you my lord bishop, welcome to Hell. What, you didn't know you were coming here? What could possibly have made you think otherwise? Ah, you mean all that fine talk of compromise, via media and "generous orthodoxy" over Visigoth and gay Rites and queer marriages with women in the kitchen and boys in the bed...such sweet music to our ears bishop. Your confreres await you."

The notion that God loves absolutely everybody, Teufel, violates the whole notion of total obedience. The freedom of the Will to willfully abandon His commandments and the need for radical discipleship seems lost on these poor fools. The deeper truth, Teufel, is that they were never His in the first place. They mistakenly thought that throwing a little water over them and saying a few words admitted them into His family, when in fact it was only a down payment for future promises of total surrender. It never happened. Their notion of baptism is little more than ecclesiastical gerrymandering. The floors of hell are paved with liberals, progressives, revisionists and Affirming Catholics.

Now make sure that lawsuits follow swiftly and painfully in South Carolina. This will brilliantly deflect from their mission and calling. It is a marvelously distracting moment and can run for weeks, months and even years, leaving little time to talk about Him and his life-saving Gospel. Distraction is the name of the game, Teufel.

We were delighted to learn that recent polls show a growing majority of Americans no longer feel comfortable with words like "sin". Such a word is highly offensive to defenders of the Sexual Revolution; the mere mention of the word creates apoplexy. My, how times have changed, Teufel, and to our advantage, no less. We much prefer words like "dysfunction"... far more satisfying.

There was a time when preachers and pastors railed against sin and evil and the darkness that followed and then the free offer of salvation and hope. No more. What traditional Christians have believed for 2,000 years about sexual behavior is now considered narrow and intolerant. So-called Christian denominations like The Episcopal Church are content to rewrite the rules even as they diminish and decline. What were once simply mainstream evangelical expressions of sexual morality have now been marginalized and degraded. It is sweet music to our ears, Teufel.

Remember that the immortal words of Yogi Berra, "It ain't over till it's over" still ring true. The other side has an arsenal of possibilities. When people are down and out, they turn to Him for rescue and guidance, not us. When the storms and thunder clouds roll and children are slaughtered by their mad gun laws, they turn to Him for solace. Such random acts of violence rarely benefit us. The one lonely gun-slinging soul who makes his way here is vastly offset by the knowledge that children wing their way to heaven and to their Father. Our Father goes mad with rage.

Choose your battles carefully, Teufel. Don't overplay your hand. We love moderate men of all shades of opinion, agnostics and skeptics who are not sure He exists, atheists who deny him and materialists who concern themselves with only their own comfort unmindful of the life to come. The Hawkins and the Dawkins are sweet music to our ears. Blot out the future, Teufel. Make them think only of the present...starve their souls. Then they are ours.

I remain your affectionate uncle,

Faust

PANSEXUALITY, DISSIMULATION AND SUBTERFUGE

My dear Teufel,

It is hard to fathom, even by our standards of dissimulation and subterfuge, just how fast western culture is moving in our direction.

We have gone from the love that dare not speak its name to full acceptance of homoerotic behavior declaring all opposition to pansexuality as homophobic and hate speech. That same sex marriage is being endorsed in state after state in the Disunited States is most comforting especially with only token opposition from the Roman Catholic Church and a few evangelicals.

The speed with which this is being accomplished has been stunning in its swiftness and fulfillment. Our Father's glee is only matched by his desire for even greater results.

The Church remains our greatest challenge and our Father's deepest, abiding hatred. Even as darkness descends over the West, the powerful resurgence of Christianity in Africa and Latin America continues apace threatening all our work. The rise of Christianity in China is causing our Father apoplectic fits.

That African Anglicans are now sending their missionaries into what was once the Christian West in an attempt to reconvert the West deeply angers our Father who has effectively used sodomy to stifle Muslim evangelization.

This new pope is terrifyingly humble and personable with a faith that ordinary people can identify with. This new Anglican fellow Justin Welby is the worst of the worst; he's an evangelical who actually believes their vile gospel. We could be undone even as the Spongs, Robinsons, Inghams, Jefferts Schoris and their revisionist ilk kill off the last vestiges of faith in North American Anglicanism.

Even atheism is falling on hard times with unbelievers squabbling among themselves over the limits of unbelief.

Richard Dawkins, one of our more adorable atheist candidates for the pit, actually admitted he was a "cultural Anglican," and liked the Church of England around if only for cultural reasons. This is the thin end of the wedge, Teufel. Any concession to the other side allows room for belief and that is disastrous. There must be no concessions, Teufel. None. Any rays of spiritual light must be met with the thunderstorms of skepticism and doubt with appeals to scientific rationalism and the Big Bang theory.

The church is filled with moderate men and women of all shades of opinion who pose no threat to the other side but is sweet music to our ears. Parsing the strict claims of the gospel, watering it down to fit the urges and compulsions of the times in which we live is precisely what we want. We want people to hedge their bets, preach inclusion and diversity. We want them to play the compassion card, the poor me's - an all loving God who allows humans to do whatever they want with their bodies because they say so is precisely the way to go. Let them play on His presumption, Teufel. Make people believe that God has changed His mind for them. Use some of those passages in the O.T. about where God repented of what he had done. Never mind that they misuse the texts to suit their tastes, the important thing to remember is that they must never compromise their positions or they will be forced to repent. That would be a total disaster for our side and bring down our Father's wrath on both of us, and we have seen what he can do when he is in one of his wrathful moods.

Remember, never overplay your hand, Teufel. You have done this on occasion resulting in a backlash of conversions that has sent our Father on drinking fits, mainly quaffing down large pints of bishops' blood which only makes him even angrier as the stuff tastes like a cross between used cassocks and stale miters. Unbelief is a heady tonic. Bishops' blood tastes like hell after a couple of decades. Bishop Pike lost a lot in the deserts of Arabia, if I recall.

Keep human happiness in the forefront of people's minds. Let them believe that to eat drink and be merry is the highest pleasure, that self-indulgence and freedom to do what you like in the name of personal fulfillment is what all humans seek. Let all talk of the "other" be just that...talk. Such liberal notions are not grounded in actuality but in the fantasy that they can really change the world. MDGs and the Five

Marks of Mission keep people from examining their own hearts and consciences, throwing themselves into lofty causes about what ought to be done to save the planet diverts them from the inner need for repentance.

Keep the whole panoply of new age nonsense squarely in people's sights. That eros, not agape, is the highest and greatest love. Let Deepak and Oprah be the guiding lights with a sprinkling of Obama "The One" and Pelosi adding political nostrums, condoms and abortifacients for all. The Nones are our future leading to a fully existential world with a gaping spiritual vacuum that we will fill with sex, drugs and rock-n-roll. The moment the Millennials tire of these things we have a problem. Prepare Plan B.

Meantime, remember just as Rome and Greece fell, so too will the US, the greatest show on earth. We are bankrupting it from the inside out. This has resulted in a lower birth rate, the rise of Islam (in time a much longed for caliphate,) the poor getting poorer, the rich getting richer, and the middle class slowly being squeezed into poverty. Education is being denuded of moral values. The "me" generation now has Facebook and Twitter, cell phones and iPads to while away the hours, unmindful of the state of their souls.

Those recent bombings by militant Islamists only hurts the long-term solutions we seek as they bring people together; worse, they may even revive faith, a truly horrible thought, Teufel. Punish those who do these things as they do not help us in the cause of dissimulation and disintegration. Remember denying the truth about Him and the meaning of life is not our goal. We can never win that one. Distorting the truth, turning truth on its head, and twisting truth to make it mean what we want it to mean is the goal.

Remember the other side still retains great resources at their disposal. One of the worst is that when these vile humans come to an end of themselves, they are vulnerable to belief. When they repent, our Father drowns his sorrows in more bishops' blood.

Drunks and bums, sodomites and fornicators, adulterers and drug addicts, tax cheaters and frauds make the best converts for the other side when the light bulbs of forgiveness and grace are turned on.

Conversely, self-righteous clergy, self-satisfied smug bishops and archbishops who lead their flocks astray are sweet music to our ears. Encourage them with more possibilities of power and attainment of full acceptance by their peers if they roll over to our side. Whisper in their ears that all is well and that they are doing His will when really they are doing ours.

Remember millions of souls are at stake and everyone that embraces the dark side, however dressed up in purple, lace and ermine, succumbs to our hell.

Our Father sends his very warmest greetings,

Your affectionate uncle,

Faust

CIVIL PARTNERSHIPS AND THE BOY SCOUTS OF AMERICA

My dear Teufel,

The collective heads of the Hades High Council is positively spinning with all the news of these foolish earthlings in their desire to find peace, harmony, love and "why can't we all get along" interfaith notions.

Their compromises over pansexual behavior have to be one of the single greatest triumphs of the 21st Century. Our Father had to be dragged away from a round of bishop bashing just to hear the good news.

Now that both the Archbishops of Canterbury and York have succumbed to the notion of civil partnerships while condemning gay marriage is of course the thin end of the wedge. Sodomy is sodomy. Recognizing it must have caused heartburn to the Enemy whose standards of holiness and righteousness cause vomiting fits among the High Council.

We are winning the Culture Wars with the help of the churches, an outstanding achievement, Teufel, one that no doubt would have had a

Cranmer, Luther or Calvin rolling in their graves. The very fact that the churches are assisting us is simply more proof that undermining is a far better policy than direct confrontation. Their misplaced compassion has worked totally to our advantage. Feel the pain of an aggrieved minority about whatever, set them up in front of television cameras to tell their story, let the public feel their pain, and hey, presto, we have more converts. Television has dumbed down entire generations causing short term memory and the impossibility of thinking in logical categories.

The Boy Scout decision is a triumph of moral and sexual disorder the likes of which we could not have envisioned in such a short space in time. Buggery in the pup tents and no one will dare report it for fear of being called homophobic. What poor fools they are. They have succumbed to the notion of inclusivity and diversity and played right into our hands. The speed with which all this is occurring is beyond even what we could have imagined. It is as though General Paton had ridden his tanks right into Berlin while Adolph and Eva were still eating Bratwurst for breakfast. Such a triumph among pubescent Boy Scouts experimenting with sex in the name of inclusion and diversity is beyond whatever we could have imagined so quickly.

The Gay PR lobby must be kept stoked with money and aggrieved anger with attendant cries of homophobia and hate to any real or imagined opposition. Let them never rest from their imagined fears that there are those out to kill them. It is a lie of course, but such lies work to our advantage. This Gene Robinson fellow keeps running around the world saying he was going to be killed at his consecration. It is a lie, of course. The security was tighter than a duck's backside, but the lies feed his "pain" and he gets sympathy and finally, acceptance. The design, formula and implementation are almost perfect.

We have almost seduced the entire West over sodomy and the holdouts are now pitifully small. Millenials have almost universally accepted the idea of gay marriage and children being raised in same sex unions. Of course, it is important that the medical facts of anal sex be kept from them with its 27 known STD's, the fact that more people are getting HIV/AIDS daily, and many of the drugs are no longer doing their proper job of healing. Every death is precious to our father, the Enemy mourns the losses; we gleefully cheer the gains.

Keep pushing the gay button in England, Teufel. Make sure that Dean Jeffrey John gets the miter in Monmouth. He can then link hands with Robinson and Mary Glasspool, hands and poofs across the seas.

Sowing disorder is the first order of business. We must keep from everyone that same-sex marriage harms marriage for everyone, and is particularly bad for children. These poor fools don't see the damage that redefining marriage does to religious freedom. At bottom, even the defense of religious liberty is a struggle over what is true and false about the meaning of marriage.

Should the truth about marriage-that it unites men and women so that children will have fathers and mothers-be defied by the laws of the land, we cannot expect the religious freedom of those who believe in that ancient truth to be respected under the new dominion of falsehood. That's the secret, Teufel that must be kept from the pseudo intellectuals of sodomy.

After all, if redefining marriage to include same-sex couples accords with justice and moral truth, there is no good reason for the new legal order to make room for "conscientious" religious dissenters, for clearly their consciences are malformed and unworthy of respect. Thus the fate of religious freedom, for scores of millions of Americans, stands or falls with the fate of conjugal marriage.

Any meaningful accommodation of religious freedom in the recent legislative enactments of same-sex marriage in various states must be wiped out.

The victorious legislators either do not see the conflict, don't care about it, or actually welcome its arrival, relishing the further victories yet to come over the "bigotry" of religious dissenters. The situation is dire indeed for the Enemy. Keep pushing for the full acceptance of pansexuality at all levels of church and state. Undermine traditional marriage. America is now post Protestant, almost post-Christian. Millenials have been so dumbed down by television they will believe almost anything we sell them. Hollywood has been our biggest success story. Let the new emerging generations tweet and twitter, but never come to knowledge of the truth.

While no one thinks that any state could constitutionally coerce dissenting ministers, imams, rabbis, or priests into presiding over same-sex wedding ceremonies or commandeer their sacred places of worship for such ceremonies, we know it is only a matter of time when they WILL be forced to do so. Look what happened to women's ordination in The Episcopal Church. First it happened illegally pushed by a bisexual New York bishop; then it was brokered in with the consciences of those who did not agree temporarily recognized; then that dreadful Harris woman compelled coercion in all dioceses and the jig was up.

Most of the orthodox have left TEC for new spiritual pastures -- pastures that Agent Slubrose is working overtime to subvert.

Only the monolithic Roman Catholic and Orthodox churches stand in the way of a complete takeover of the Church. The nightmare of growing Christianity in Africa and China bedevils our father. He has sent agents to persecute them. But we have learned that the Enemy can turn persecution into new conversions, much to our father's chagrin. He flames at the very thought.

We have almost routed Christianity in Mideast countries like Iran, Iraq, Syria, Israel and Egypt. Token resistance remains. India and Japan still have token Christian churches. We have corrupted the Church of South India to the point of spiritual impotency.

Our father was delighted to learn that there was a gay mafia in the Vatican with priests hooking up via social networking. This is a good start, but expand it, Teufel, and hook them up with Episcopalians and other sympatico Western Protestant liberals.

Our father is a great admirer of your handiwork. He speaks glowingly of your achievements to the High Council. Your successes are mine.

I remain your affectionate uncle,

Faust

AMERICANS REDEFINE MARRIAGE

My dear Teufel,

Word has reached us that you have added a significant skull to your belt. The Americans have changed the definition of marriage, redefined it to accommodate same-sex couples, reinforcing the idea that marriage is irrelevant to parenthood. An excellent accomplishment, Teufel. That three percent of the population managed to hoodwink the other 97% into thinking they can change the ontology and cosmology of marriage is a brilliant achievement by any standard. I have never seen our Father in a more gleeful state. The Enemy must be in tears.

And, having done so, those poor foolish Episcopalians rang the bells at their national cathedral (how ironic to call it a "National House of Prayer") to celebrate sodomite marriages. I can assure you their prayers descended not ascended. I must tell you, however, that Hells Bells put them to shame. WE know for whom the bells toll...

Of course, we know that this great day in American history has absolutely nothing to do with "equal rights" or "gender equality." How could it? Homosexuals comprise a mere three percent of the population, yet you and the other demons have managed to cause an entire nation to redefine traditional marriage between a man and a woman; and the idiots on the Supreme Court, besotted by the culture, went for it. Only that Scalia fellow didn't fall for it. See that he is marginalized as an out of touch justice and fundamentalist Catholic. Of course, all this is possible because our father - the Father of Lies - through your help, made it all possible.

By redefining marriage, same-sex marriage will lead to the casualization of heterosexual unions and ultimately separate marriage and parenthood. See to it that in the move towards same-sex marriage, opposite-sex relationships have to conform to gay norms rather than the other way around. Hollywood has glamorized fornication though no one talks about disease and suicide.

Never mind that across all countries analyzed no causal link has ever been established to support the idea that same-sex marriage prevents marital decline. Never let the facts get in the way of pansexual cultural advancement. Cement it all, Teufel.

We were doubly delighted to learn that after being notified of the Supreme Court's ruling, the president made a congratulatory call from Air Force One to the plaintiffs in California's Proposition 8 case, a call that was also broadcast on MSNBC, the unofficial mouthpiece for the administration. He is clearly the most pro Muslim, anti-Christian president ever and is pro-gay marriage as well. By supporting the overturn of the democratically passed Prop. 8 in California, he has shown his real colors, if you'll pardon the pun.

Our Father is putting out a new welcome mat, "Welcome to American Babylon, 2013."

Keep up the systematic attack on the moral fabric of the nation, Teufel. The internal takeover of America is your primary concern; the rest will follow. Forcing the acceptance of same-sex unions is part of a larger plan that our Father outlined and detailed nearly a century ago through the Marxist philosopher Antonio Gramsci. His theory of cultural hegemony describes the domination of a culturally diverse society by the ruling class, who manipulate the culture of the society - the beliefs, explanations, perceptions, values, and mores - so that the ruling-class becomes the worldview that is imposed and accepted as the cultural norm.

These foolish Americans don't read history. They spend their waking hours, when not working on mindless sports, killing themselves on fast food and cheap booze. Lull them all with late night porn. Keep the more intelligent ones talking about interfaith stuff.... such sweet music to our Father's ears.

Keep up the attack on children. The children of the U.S. are considered to be one of the most important "resources" for the takeover of America. See that the schools keep pushing pansexuality, infiltrate them with our newer younger agents preparing them for a world without Him, a world of so-called tolerance and blind acceptance of the New Order we are establishing.

At the same time curriculums of moral corruption are being taught in their schools, the removal of God is necessary as it is antithetical to the debauchery of tolerance and acceptance that we are pushing. It is not without its significance that kids from Christian homes and churches soon lose their faith when they enter college and university. Spread it like a cancer, Teufel.

The end game is approaching. Legalizing same-sex sexual activity and marriage is but one of numerous attacks our Father is planning and you must initiate against America from within. Along with the Balkanization of America, the end game is secularization -- the complete loss of transcendence, the humanization and destruction of the moral heritage of the nation. It really doesn't matter if you are a Democrat or a Republican, we have seduced politicians on both sides of the political divide.

Mind how you go with the political and social agenda of the LGBTQI movement colliding with the freedom of religion guaranteed all Americans in the US Constitution. Things could backfire. A couple of recent court rulings demonstrate that an undercurrent of righteousness still exists and can work against us.

Remember that the booming self-help industry along with New Age spirituality has the message we love which is to be authentic: Live fully. Realize yourself. Be connected. Achieve well-being. Above all, play down any talk of the Enemy as necessary for their salvation. The Millenials are all but ours. However, never forget the Enemy has resources that keep our father in a permanently restless state.

Nonetheless, our father is so proud of your achievement, he is thinking of making you principal of the School of Demons Officially Family Friendly (SODOFF) next summer (during the hot season) to train a new generation of demons for the fall. Keep up the good work.

I remain your affectionate uncle,

Faust

MY INTERVIEW TO BE THE NEXT BISHOP OF MUDDY WATERS, WEST VIRGINIA

PANEL: Before we even consider you for bishop Dr. Virtue we need to vet you for your views.

VOL: I wouldn't have it any other way.

PANEL: What do you think of women?

VOL: I rather like them. I have been married to one for over 30 years and as far as I can make she is still speaking to me.

PANEL: What about your views of women in ministry?

VOL: I'm for women deacons but no higher in the pecking order. I do believe women deacons should wear their cassocks right down to the ground, you have no idea what a well-turned ankle can do to excite lust in my heart.

PANEL: Excellent response. What about your views on gays.

VOL: Know a few, like a few and my brother-in-law was happy.

PANEL: We mean Gay...

VOL: ...gay meaning homosexual? Got it.

PANEL: Do you think non-celibate gays should be ordained?

VOL: Absolutely not. The Bible expressly forbids it in seven places. Sexuality is viewed as a creation ordinance, that cannot be changed, however hard people try.

PANEL: What was the name of that book again?

VOL: The Bible.

PANEL: Of course. So, you are not inclusive then?

VOL: That all depends on what you mean by the word "inclusive". The Bible never includes sinful sexual behavior as an option. The only sex it recognizes is sex between a man and a woman in marriage. No options or alternatives.

PANEL: Isn't that rather narrow?

VOL: Jesus said, "Enter through the narrow gate. For wide is the gate and broad is the road that leads to destruction, and many enter." I'm with the few not the many.

PANEL: What are your views on diversity.

VOL: If it means tolerance for people of different backgrounds, ethnic diversity, the acceptance of multiple ethnic cultures and cultural diversity, respect of different cultures and interculturality, then yes. It cannot mean diversity in sexual terms. I also think it applies to flower arrangements.

PANEL What is your view on "good disagreement" advocated by the Archbishop of Canterbury?

VOL: That's like pouring arsenic onto an ice cream cone in the hope that you'll like it.

PANEL: What is your view of the Church embracing transgendered priests?

VOL: I would become a dispensationalist and believe the end is nigh.

PANEL: What is your take on the Presiding Bishops' "Jesus Movement"?

VOL: I had no idea Jesus had moved. I thought he was "the same, yesterday, today and forever."

PANEL: How would you define your episcopacy should you be elected?

VOL: First of all, I would throw out all practicing sodomites. Engaging in unhealthy and life-threatening sex is a sin and not an option. Repentance is called for. I would reinforce gospel proclamation. Demand that priests actually read the Bible and pray every day. Get priests to start talking about sin and salvation and advocate against racism once a year. Dump White Privilege talk and preach up discipleship and what it REALLY means to follow Jesus. Also live more simply. Stop buying stuff you don't need. Give more to charities that genuinely help people and charge priests to get involved in at least one ministry outside their church.

PANEL: Excellent. We will recommend you for Bishop of Muddy Waters, West Virginia.

VOL: But there is no such see!

PANEL: That's why we are recommending you.

SEXUAL REVOLUTION HAS WORKED OUT WELL, EPISCOPAL CHURCH PRIMATE REPORTS

Reflecting on the Sexual revolution begun in the U.S. in the 60's, Episcopal Presiding Bishop Michael Curry told a hastily called press conference that it has worked well for his church citing the magnificent efforts of bi-sexual bishops like Paul Moore and Gene Robinson who managed to pull the Church into the 20th and 21st centuries and out of the 19th century and quite possibly the first.

"They were pioneers and prophets, bringing their sexual talents to bare at a time when so many were doing it in the closet. We are now a church full of perverts and sex weirdos that we have literally caught up with the culture and may have even surpassed it. Changing our canons on marriage was a game changer. God has blessed us with an ever expanding and financially growing Church Pension Fund to take us to the next levels of transgenderism and beyond to those people who believe that they must have BOTH a penis and a vagina. I am in awe of our future."

"It's historic," opined the Presiding Bishop. "Old fashioned adultery and fornication, bullying, lying and stealing was not enough, we needed the full range of LGBTQXXXxxx1212 sexualities to sweep the Church and we have been successful. Praise the Lord and let us thank Rumi the Sufi, a favorite guru of Frank Griswold. Along with the last three presiding bishops' we have managed to throw off the shackles of biblical morality."

In a panegyric of praise to TEC, Curry said, "We have made unbridled passion the cornerstone of the Church and with it pansexual liberation. It is a glorious time to be alive and an Episcopalian. My real hope in 2018, is to export our sexuality practices to the Global South and those sad, backward fundamentalists in GAFCON."

Questioned about the ongoing decline of the Episcopal Church, Curry said, God is doing a new thing but he wasn't quite sure what it is, but we would all find out soon enough. "I am putting my money on anti-racism and white privilege in a church that is 98% white."

With his eyes cast towards the blinding sun, Curry said he wanted all Episcopalians to have a blessed Christmas, a wonderful New Year, and go out, in the name of the Jesus Movement and make disciples of the LGBTQ community and if you can't save them, join them and tell them they are part of "beloved community", even if it means moving the goalposts so no one ever actually gets saved.

END

PROFILING

The following events are cuts from contemporary ecclesiastical history. They actually happened. The following is a multiple-choice test which you can take. There is only one right answer.

1.   Who was failed by his examining chaplains for postulancy to the priesthood, but whose mother got him into seminary anyway?
      a.   St. Augustine
      b.   Athanasius
      c.   Calvin
      d.   Luther
      e.   Cranmer
      f.   Hooker
      g.   Episcopal Bishop Charles E. Bennison

2.   Who believes the Church wrote the bible and can therefore rewrite it?
      a.   St. Paul
      b.   Augustine
      c.   Luther
      d.   Karl Barth
      e.   Thomas Jefferson
      f.   Episcopal Bishop Charles E. Bennison

3.   Who believes that Jesus is "a Christ" but not the Christ?
    a.   Gregory of Nyssa
    b.   Arius (close but no cigar)
    c.   Sun Myung Moon
    d.   Shirley Maclaine
    e.   Madonna/Esther
    f.   Episcopal Bishop Charles E. Bennison

4.   Who believes that Jesus is a forgiven sinner and not sinless?
    a.   St. Paul
    b.   Augustine
    c.   Wesley
    d.   Ted Kennedy
    e.   Jesse Jackson
    f.   Bill Clinton
    g.   Episcopal Bishop Charles E. Bennison

5.   Who believes that the new ECUSA religion IS clearly superior to the 'faith once delivered' to the saints?
    a.   Mary Baker Eddy
    b.   Joseph Smith
    c.   Jimmy Swaggart
    d.   Episcopal Bishop Charles E. Bennison

6.   Who believes that when Jesus said "who do men say that I am"
that he was searching for his own personal identity?

    a.   Robin Williams

    b.   Jonathan Winters

    c.   Bob Newhart

    d.   Sigmund Freud

    e.   Mel Brooks

    f.   Episcopal Bishop Charles E. Bennison

7.   Who believes that the growth of the Church in Africa can be
equated to the growth of the Nazi Party?

    a.   Adolph Hitler

    b.   Adolph Eichmann

    c.   Joseph Goebbels

    d.   Charles de Gaulle

    e.   Winston Churchill

    f.   Saddam Hussein

    g.   Osama Bin Laden

    h.   Episcopal Bishop Charles E. Bennison

8.   Who thinks you can write a Visigoth Rite for marriages that
replaces the ancient liturgies of the church and what the Bible
declares about marriage between a man and a woman?

    a.   St. Paul

    b.   Origen

    c.   Athanasius

    d.   Garrison Keiller

    e.   A Norwegian from Minnesota

    f.   A Viking

    g.   Episcopal Bishop Charles E. Bennison

9.   Who out of personal frustration with an orthodox rector misuses the canons of the church in an attempt to strong arm that rector out of the church?

    a.   St. Paul

    b.   St. Augustine

    c.   Pope Leo X

    d.   Ethelbert the Ignorant

    e.   Henry VIII

    f.   Episcopal Bishop Charles E. Bennison

10.   Who would declare that the ministries of a properly ordained Anglo-Catholic priest could be invalidated by not adhering to a revisionist bishop on matters of faith and order?

    a.   St Peter

    b.   Athanasius

    c.   Pope John Paul II

    d.   Puff Daddy

    e.   Episcopal Bishop Charles E. Bennison

11.   Who believes that a revisionist bishop who doesn't believe in the Deity of Christ can tell an orthodox priest that he is administering the sacraments invalidly?

    a.   Pope John Paul II

    b.   Bishop Keith Ackerman

    c.   The Russian Patriarch

    d.   The Coptic Patriarch

    e.   Episcopal Bishop Charles E. Bennison

12.   Who believes that sodomy is good and right in the eyes of God, and will happily marry most sexual arrangements in his cathedral?

    a.   Richard Simmons

    b.   Sitting Bull

    c.   The Supreme Court of Massachusetts

    d.   Butch Cassidy

    e.   The Lutheran Church Missouri Synod

    f.   The Roman Catholic Church

    g.   Episcopal Bishop Charles E. Bennison

13.   Who believes that sodomy is an acceptable sexual behavior?

    a.   The World Wrestling Federation

    b.   Elmer Fudd

    c.   George W. Bush

    d.   Bonnie and Clyde

    e.   NASCAR Drivers

    f.   Captain Kangaroo

    g.   Billy Graham

    h.   Episcopal Bishop Charles E. Bennison

14.   Which revisionist bishop told an orthodox priest that you are:

    a.   Consecrating bread and wine and it is not the body and blood of Jesus.

    b.   You are baptizing children and they are not regenerate.

    c.   You are marrying people and they are not married.

    d.   You are burying people and they are not dead!!!

Scratch D.

Guess?

Nope, I really don't see a pattern here to justify profiling, do you? So, to ensure that Episcopalians never offend anyone, particularly pansexualists, lesbitransgay participants, gays in long term committed relationships for six months or longer, the Episcopal Church will conduct random searches for unbaptized souls and those who have not taken anti-racism training courses. In the event that they are found they will be turned over to the Presiding Bishop for punishment and charges will be brought against them by the Title IV Review Committee.

THE FIRST EPISTLE OF PRESIDING BISHOP FRANK GRISWOLD

The Word of Frank

1.That which was from the beginning, which we have heard, which we have seen with our eyes, which we have looked at and our hands have touched—this we proclaim concerning the Episcopal Church.

2. The life in ECUSA appeared for a season, we have seen it and testify to it, and we proclaim to you the brief life, all too brief, which was with Frank and appeared to the House of Bishops with much blinding and diverse light.

3. We proclaim to you what we have seen and heard, so that you also may have fellowship with us and be inclusive and not excluded, for that would be a crying shame and cause many of us to be sad, for we believe in collegiality above all else. And our fellowship is with one another and it is here that we Dance the Circle Dance of Dispossession when the House of Bishops gather, in order to dispossess ourselves of all bad thoughts and rejuvenate our karmas.

4. I write these "gracious" words to make our common joy complete.

5. This is the message we have heard from Sufi Rumi and declare unto you: Sufi is light; and in him there is no darkness at all for he dwelleth on a plain beyond good and evil where we all hope one day to dwell, for truly there is no darkness in that place.

6. If we claim to have fellowship with the beloved Sufi and yet continue to walk in the darkness of absolutism where there is no pluriform thinking, we lie and do not live by the many pluriform truths of which I am a great advocate.

7. But if we walk in the transcendent light of Sufi, as he is in the light, we have collegiality with one another; and the thoughts of Sufi Rumi purifies us from all bad thoughts and raises us up beyond good and evil so we don't have to worry about those narrow-minded orthodox types who still inhabit my church. For truly there is a GREATER truth which inhabiteth Otis of the Charles and Vickie of the Gene pool who embrace many of their own species, much to their delight and ours.

8. If we proclaim to be without error, and I am rarely wrong, we deceive ourselves only if we do not see things my way, and the truth is not in you.

9. If we confess that it is my way or it will be the highway, we will be liberated from the bondage of believing in sin which only causes us unnecessary guilt which I have banished as being bad for your karma and aura. For there are many truths and I know most of them.
10. If you have not embraced pluriform truths and wish to live in the narrow confines of single truths there will ultimately be no place for you among the House of Purple, for you will feel out of place because of your narrow-minded thinking. Therefore you will cry a lot and feel excluded, and I would not wish that.

Chapter 2

1. My dear ECUSANs, I write this to you so that you will not fall into the habit of believing in personal sin, for truly there are only bad thoughts and they can be brushed aside if you perform acts of mercy. Think good thoughts, for I have banished the bad and the attendant guilt. If you do have bad thoughts speak to me and I will absolve you of all psychological guilt feelings, for that is all they are. And I will speak to Sufi in your defense for he is the Righteous One.

2. And there is no need for atonement, for Mel (Gibson) doth have it wrong. Think triumphantly and you will be triumphant. Think good thoughts and goodness will flow from you.

3. For truly if you obey me, you will be right, and things will go smoothly for you.

4. The bishop who says "I know you, Frank" but does not do what I command is a liar and shall receive a private visit from David Booth Beers and he WILL demonstrate that the truth is not in you, and verily he will invoke the Dennis Canon and you shall be very much afraid. I, Frank have spoken and my words will not be gracious unto you.

5. But if everyone obeys my word, my love and that of Sufi Rumi will be made complete with a large and bounteous check from the many and diverse Trust Funds that I have at my disposal, and verily you shall never go without. That is how you know you belong to me.

6. Whoever claims to live in me, must walk as I do, and good things shall flow bounteously from me to you, and you shall want for nothing.

7. Dear friends, none of this is new, for I have been preaching pluriformity for years, it is very old and goes back to Lambeth '98 where I made public my 'pluriform truths' speech at a press conference. This is old news, but let me refresh you just in case you don't get the message and ill befalls you.

8. Yet in a way I am writing you a new command; its truth is seen in me and my revisionist pals in the HoB, because the old exclusive, fundamentalist, narrow 'light' of the gospel is slowly being extinguished and the new light of Sufi Rumi shineth, and this light inhabiteth me and it will, if you accept it and come with me to a plain beyond good and evil, find yourself shining as the noonday sun passing over a gay bathhouse in Niagara, New York which was closed down for it was no longer a 'safe place' and many did catch the dreaded disease.

9. Anyone who claims to be in the light, and I hope that is all 100 diocesan bishops, but still loves orthodoxy, is still in the darkness.

10. Whoever loves his brother bishop (and you have your choice of eros, philia, storge or agape, but Frankly I prefer the first), will not cause his fellow bishop to stumble, otherwise he will be forced to stand in a corner at an Oasis meeting in the Diocese of Newark and there have his bottom smacked by Louie of the Earnest.

11. But whoever hates his brother bishop is in the darkness and walks around in the darkness and he will no longer Dance the Circle Dance of Dispossession with us and will find (Sufi forbid), a presentment against him and face the wrath of his fellow bishops, because it is very clear the darkness of narrow-minded orthodoxy has blinded him.

12. I write to you dear children of ECUSA, because I want to banish all bad thoughts on account of the name of my friend Sufi who knoweth all things.

13. I write to you fathers in God, because you have known me from the beginning and I can speak out of many sides of my mouth, and make words mean what I want them to mean and not mean, and when all else fails I can resolve it all in 'mystery' which we can all embrace, even as I am embraced by you. I write to you, young men, because you have overcome the narrowness of exclusive thinking. I write to you, dear children, because you are easily indoctrinated by the new thinking much proclaimed in our modern textbooks from Episcopal Publishing Houses and other publishing places of pluriformity.

Do Not Love the Orthodox

14. Do not love the orthodox or anything they believe any more. If anyone loves the orthodox, the love of myself and Sufi Rumi is not in him.

15. For everything in orthodox thinking – the cravings for absolute truth, the lust for true spirituality and the boasting of what he has and does – comes not from me and Suff, but from the Bible and that is subject to many interpretations, and I have used many in the course of my lifetime.

16. For the church, The Episcopal Church may be passing away, but the Episcopalian who does my will and that of Suff will live forever, or until the money runs out and I have to take out a mortgage on 815 2nd avenue, but that will be long after I am dead and gone to live with Rumi on his plain of happiness.

Warnings Against Orthodoxy

17. Dear children of ECUSA, many think this is the last hour of our beloved church, but it is not so. We may have a cash flow problem but it is temporary, and if the markets continue to rise we can live off the interest of the Trust Funds for years and the Church Pension Fund floweth like the Hudson River forever and ever. I may no longer travel First Class and be reduced to Business Class in my peregrinations around the globe as I promote my inclusive, affirming, pan-everything notion of mission, but I will suffer the hardship for your sake and my gospel.

18. The orthodox went out from us, but they did not really belong to us. For if they had belonged to us, they would have remained with us and believed the new religion; but their going showed that none of them REALLY belonged to us because they could not accept pluriform truths, of which I am its foremost advocate. Their very narrowness was their undoing, for they could not see the big picture which now includes Vickie of the Gene pool.

19. But you have been anointed by me when you became bishop. I laid my hands on your head and said you belonged to me and the Dennis Canon, and behold you do....until you die...or you will face the Title IV Review Committee.

20. Who is the liar? It is the bishop who denies my authority and that Suff is the Liberator of our narrowness and exclusivity. Such a man is the antiSuff, he denies me and Suff and that is unforgivable. No one who denies my inclusive thinking has Suff in him; whoever acknowledges me, Frank of the Flexible Wrist, gets a night in my New York City Penthouse, dinner at Club 21...and that's a bargain.

21. Therefore, see that what you have heard from the beginning, or 1998, remains in you. If it does, you will remain my friend forever and ever and I will be a 'safe place' for you and you shall never be attacked by narrow uninclusive bishops like Duncan of the Pitts.

22. I write so you won't be lead astray by Iker of the Fortress mentality, for the anointing you have received from me remains with you, and you do not need anyone else to teach you, for my anointing is real, not counterfeit as some wretched cyber journalist says to you. So remain in me, for I am your liberator and friend.

Fondly,

Frank

WELCOME TO THE JESUS MOVEMENT: EPISCOPAL CHURCH ANNOUNCES 2017-2018 REVIVALS

NEWS ITEM: The Episcopal Church is working with diocesan teams to organize a series of Episcopal Revivals in 2017 and 2018, six major events that promise to stir and renew hearts for Jesus, to equip Episcopalians as evangelists, and to welcome people who aren't part of a church to join the Jesus Movement.

My dear Teufel,

Agent Slubnose brought us the news today that this Michael Curry fellow who now leads the Episcopal Church is hellbent on reviving his Church in the vain hope of staving off its inevitable decline. Words like "evangelism" and "renewing hearts for Him" are not words we like to hear as they signal a possible turnaround in that Church's fortunes. However, we have been informed from other sources that we have nothing to fear, as he links it all to racism and white privilege, which is sweet music to our ears. Anything that keeps people from believing they are universally and by nature sinners and in need of a savior is to be applauded. Off road it to racism and white privilege and the game is lost. Sowing those kinds of seeds keeps them away from the essential and real news of what the Other Side really wants.

We also know that both 20/20 (to double the size of the Episcopal Church by this date) and the Task Force for Reimagining the Episcopal Church (TREC) have failed and now they are trying again to give it the old school try. Lead them along and let them believe that this time it will work. Flattery is the best form of delusion. The whole idea of revival can only come from Him, it cannot be manufactured at a so-called revival meeting.

Now it is important for Episcopalians to keep reaffirming that racism, sexism and homophobia are the real issues and that they need to label orthodox Anglicans who don't share their views as "racists," "sexists," "any-other-ists", "phobes" and haters as the true enemy of the faith. Keep toilets and transgenderism as the major whine of liberals and label those who disagree as sexual Neanderthals.

The constantly mutating laws of political correctness must be maintained at all costs.

Keep Episcopalians believing that Jesus was the closest thing to Hilary Clinton and her losing is a loss to all stripes of progressives, spiritual and political. If only Jesus was a woman, Mary Glasspool would not have had to go through all the agony of being the first lesbian bishop in the Episcopal Church.

Keep up the pipe line frenzy: Wave the flag of self-righteousness in the face of progress for everyone. Make this the new cause celebre for TEC. Let the Church be consumed with climate change, but not the cold climate in their hearts and souls. Keep finding new causes for the bishops to feel (self) righteous about. More causes, more prevarication, more delay, more sexualities to affirm and their souls are ours.

The most important thing this Curry fellow can do is to follow up on his promise in Canterbury to push his Church's progressive sexual agenda onto the Africans. This is sweet music to our ears. Make sure the money spigots are open to this invasion of sexual promiscuities in the name of "justice" and "inclusion". Never let it be said that their God is one of wrath and judgement, only that He is nice and inclusive of all.

Sear their consciences, dull their minds, but under no circumstances are they to believe that there are any consequences for their behavior.

And remember that our father's definition of a Happy New Year is more of the same, and remember Hell is full of people who not only wanted life on their own terms; in the end got it.

I remain your affectionate uncle,

Faust

EPISCOPAL PRESIDING BISHOP SAYS HE WILL REPATRIATE PARISHES WON IN LAWSUITS BACK TO ORIGINAL OWNERS

Presiding Bishop Michael Curry says he was deeply challenged by Pope Francis's action to gift a Lamborghini to help Iraqi Christians. "It touched my conscience," he said.

NEWS ITEM: Pope Francis gifted a Lamborghini supercar -- but gave it away to help Iraqi Christians. The famously ascetic pontiff publicly blessed the car but elected that it be auctioned off with the proceeds used to help Christian communities attempting to rebuild in the Middle East. The gleaming white-and-gold Lamborghini Huracán, which usually sells at around €180,000, ($212.000) was made specifically for the Pope by the car manufacturer. Pope Francis blessed the vehicle - and signed its bonnet - at the Vatican's Casa Santa Marta, according to The Telegraph.

The Presiding Bishop of the Episcopal Church, Michael Curry, said today he was deeply moved by the Pope's actions when he heard the news, and immediately called together the Executive Council for a behind closed doors meeting and later issued the following statement:

"In light of the Holy Father's actions, I, with my Executive Council and Gay Jennings, president of the House of Deputies, have decided to repatriate all those parishes we won in decades long law suits and give them back to their original and rightful owners. Furthermore, we publicly repent of our actions in spending over $40 million in court cases across the country and we vow not to take any legal complaints to the SCOTUS. We think all this litigation has gone far enough as it is beginning to affect our bottom line in dealing with serious social concerns of which we have many like transgender bathroom rulings in North Carolina and Texas."

The Presiding Bishop went on to say that racism and white privilege were his main concerns but declined to name any racists in The Episcopal Church. "It's the thought and idea that counts. In any event it is part of my ongoing Jesus Movement push which is still waiting to catch fire after three years."

He said he was off to England next month to consult with the Archbishop of Canterbury about how to get it off the ground.

"I think we can learn a lot from his desire for "good disagreement" and his push for boys who want to cross-dress, wear tutus, tiaras and high heels. I believe his call for 'Valuing all God's Children' is a game changer. I believe his Church's vote to affirm transgender people in the church, aimed at tackling homophobia and transphobia is precisely the message we want to send all Episcopalians, especially those over 65 who have never met a trannie and wouldn't know one if they fell over him/her.

"To help facilitate our willingness to drop the lawsuits, we will take all the money from the sale of 25 empty parishes in the Diocese of San Joaquin and donate it to the "Lost Boys" priests' fund who will use the money to evangelize the next generation of Sudanese into looking for the odd homosexual in Juba so they can demonstrate they are not homophobic."

WASHINGTON EPISCOPAL BISHOP HOLDS ALPHA COURSE

My dear Teufel,

We were shocked to read that the Bishop of Washington, a regular bubble brain, that we had turned to our purposes years ago was actually holding an ALPHA course in the National Cathedral. The High Council was livid when they heard the news. Several devils blew their stack. Bishop Marianne Budde is truly ours and this deviation is totally unacceptable. Our Father was not amused when he heard the news. Do you have any idea what could happen if something like this should catch fire?

Out of sheer desperation, these Episcopal bishops, who are watching as their dioceses sink into the sunset, might just go for something like this. Alpha, a course on salvation, for hell's sake...this could ruin everything!

Bishop Michael Curry's *Jesus Movement* is as faux as a knock-off Rolex watch. It's not real evangelism at all. Our Father below made sure that it would be a counterfeit evangelism, parroting the real thing but missing the mark with no real call for repentance and faith in Him. We made sure that the presiding bishop's being black would be the real issue coupled with white privilege…a form of inverted narcissism. It is really being all about him and not about Him.

Our Father, the master tactician, brilliantly allows a distorted image to mirror the real thing.

This, of course, is the genius of evil; it can masquerade as light appearing as an angel at times, when in fact darkness lurks at the edges waiting to pounce and swallow up the vulnerable and lost.

With just a small handful of holdouts the whole Episcopal House of Bishops is effectively now ours and what a house of cards it is. They have fallen for the oldest trick in the book, 'ye shall be as gods' without knowing good from evil. They have embraced the unembraceable and in doing so embraced us.

The culture wars are almost over - and we have won. The mainline Protestant denominations have nearly all rolled over on sodomy and homosexual marriage and now this transgendered nonsense. It is quite possibly the best public relations coup by pansexualists in modern history. We are even making inroads into the Roman Catholic Church, something we never thought possible. The thin end of the wedge was the sexual abuse of young men by sodomite priests. We carefully labeled it pedophilia to put straights off the scent, but one or two activist laymen have caught on much to our annoyance.

But the language of inclusion, diversity, generous orthodoxy and now "radical inclusion" by the Archbishop of Canterbury, is a throw-back to that Griswold fellow who ran The Episcopal Church for eight years, was indeed sweet music to our Father below ears.

We first thought Welby would be a hard nut to crack as he claimed to be an evangelical, but we turned out to be gayly wrong. As it happened he was an easy mark, and roll over he did. These poor foolish bishops lack serious theological training, are doctrinally light and become easy knockoffs over time as the culture changes…they just change with it. Even the Southern Baptist Convention leaders now admit their own people don't have enough bible or history in them to resist the temptations of the world, the flesh and us. Postmodernism is our victory roll.

This Mohler fellow said evangelicals are too tied to this "particular moment in history" to find timeless roots. He is right, of course. And then he said this, "I do not believe evangelicalism has sufficient resources for a thick enough Christianity to survive either this epoch or much beyond." Precisely our point, Wormwood, and you must see that people spend their waking hours twittering and tweeting, texting and gaming. Keep them from thinking about their souls and their eternal destiny. Fritter and twitter Wormwood, fritter and twitter.

The open embrace of sin as righteousness is our ultimate goal; the complete turning of evil on its head and presenting it as truth is our victory roll. The next big push for our junior devils who are even now hard at work, is Africa and China. Our Father below was mortified to learn that China now had over 100 million Christians! Remember that persecution does not play well. It is a two-way street. We imprison, maim and kill and they become martyrs and more become Christians.

Let the goal be materialism and the good life…the pursuit of happiness for its own sake.

We have managed to persuade the political elite to eat their young by not biologically reproducing and spiritual reproduction is also at an all-time low. Our Father applauds your efforts but remember things can turn on a dime. The opposition always has a card or two up His sleeves and this Budde incident could easily flower into something dangerously like revival, a foul word that gives our Father heartburn.

See that it does not recur.

I remain your affectionate uncle,

Faust

ARCHBISHOP WELBY WISHES ARCHBISHOP OKOH BON VOYAGE FROM THE ANGLICAN COMMUNION

Archbishop Justin Welby the titular head of the Church of England sent a personal Christmas message to Nigerian Primate Nicholas Okoh wishing him bon voyage from the Anglican Communion.

"You have been a thorn in my side from the first day I took office. God knows you managed to successfully get rid of my predecessor Rowan Williams, a good and godly Hegelian Primate and now it seems you are doing everything in your power to get rid of me.

"The worst of it, is because you won't waffle and play nice over gay men who love each other and just want to be accepted for who they are. Where is your compassion one must ask? What's a little sodomy between friends in a committed relationship. Have you no heart for men who desire men even if the Bible expressly forbids it!

"Good heavens, we bought you the gospel way back when, and now you want to return the favor and plant your GAFCON flag here in Britain, the Mother Church...what the blazes are you thinking!

"The fact that you think we have lost the plot, doesn't mean you have a right to tell us where we have gone wrong. Who do you think you are? Why do you think I engineered hiring Josiah Idouw-Fearon, one of your archbishops, to man the Anglican Communion office. You think that just happened by chance? I thought this one through very carefully...and we thought you'd bite on that. But no, you saw right through me, and I went to Eton and Trinity College, Cambridge, where were you educated pray tell?

"You think you know more than me? You are the son of a peasant farmer, which is just about as bad as being the son of a Galilean carpenter, for goodness sake.

"Look here my good man, if you continue to make inroads into my church and start sheep stealing I am going to have to report you to the Queen who is the head of our church, and believe me you don't want to cross her. She can be as mean as a Muslim cleric when she gets her temper up. Just ask Prince Philip, the poor man just can't catch a break. Just watch a few episodes of The Crown.

"My final word is this, if you don't invite me to GAFCON III in Jerusalem next year, I won't invite you to the next Lambeth conference in 2020, let's see how that makes you feel."

Meantime, wishing you and yours a happy Boko Haram encounter this Christmas,

+Justin Cantuar

SEXUAL REVOLUTION HAS WORKED OUT WELL, EPISCOPAL CHURCH PRIMATE REPORTS

Reflecting on the Sexual revolution begun in the U.S. in the 60's, Episcopal Presiding Bishop Michael Curry told a hastily called press conference that it has worked well for his church citing the magnificent efforts of bi-sexual bishops like Paul Moore and Gene Robinson who managed to pull the Church into the 20th and 21st centuries and out of the 19th century and quite possibly the first.

"They were pioneers and prophets, bringing their sexual talents to bare at a time when so many were doing it in the closet. We are now a church full of perverts and sex weirdos that we have literally caught up with the culture and may have even surpassed it. Changing our canons on marriage was a game changer. God has blessed us with an ever expanding and financially growing Church Pension Fund to take us to the next levels of transgenderism and beyond to those people who believe that they must have BOTH a penis and a vagina. I am in awe of our future."

"It's historic," opined the Presiding Bishop. "Old fashioned adultery and fornication, bullying, lying and stealing was not enough, we needed the full range of LGBTQXXXxxx1212 sexualities to sweep the Church and we have been successful. Praise the Lord and let us thank Rumi the Sufi, a favorite guru of Frank Griswold. Along with the last three presiding bishops' we have managed to throw off the shackles of biblical morality."

In a panegyric of praise to TEC, Curry said, "We have made unbridled passion the cornerstone of the Church and with it pansexual liberation. It is a glorious time to be alive and an Episcopalian. My real hope in 2018, is to export our sexuality practices to the Global South and those sad, backward fundamentalists in GAFCON."

Questioned about the ongoing decline of the Episcopal Church, Curry said, God is doing a new thing but he wasn't quite sure what it is, but we would all find out soon enough. "I am putting my money on anti-racism and white privilege in a church that is 98% white."

With his eyes cast towards the blinding sun, Curry said he wanted all Episcopalians to have a blessed Christmas, a wonderful New Year, and go out, in the name of the Jesus Movement and make disciples of the LGBTQ community and if you can't save them, join them and tell them they are part of "beloved community", even if it means moving the goalposts so no one ever actually gets saved.

DIOCESE OF PENNSYLVANIA NOMINATES RECOVERING PEDOPHILE TO BE NEXT BISHOP

The Diocese of Pennsylvania's Standing Committee will recommend to its priests, parishes and parishioners the Rev. Todd Bangerboy to be the next bishop of the Diocese. He is presently a priest in the Diocese of Newark, which has some 30 homosexual and lesbian priests adorning its pulpits. His resume says he has deep interpersonal skills and relates well to young people.

"I can hardly contain myself," said Katharine Jefferts Schori, the Church's presiding bishop, upon hearing the news.

"As you know, I received into the Episcopal Church a known (and forgiven) pedophile former Roman Catholic monk Bede Parry who had been kicked out of his Church. I was hoping to put forward his name except he had the misfortune of dying.

"On another occasion I allowed a convicted and defrocked pedophile Episcopal priest to conduct spiritual retreats - two of them in an

Episcopal facility with my blessing. To be truly inclusive we must be open about God's mission to absolutely everybody."

The Presiding Bishop pooh-poohed the 74th General Convention's passage (overwhelmingly) of resolution B008 titled "Protect Children and Youth from Abuse".

"This resolution is like DOMA and must be repealed, it has gone the way of the Dodo bird," opined the Presiding Bishop.

"We are an inclusive church," commented former New Hampshire Bishop Gene Robinson. "I am overwhelmed at the forgiveness of God. What a magnificent person She is. Fr Bangerboy will be up for the job, I'm sure."

Questioned on the possibility of recidivism among pedophiles, Standing Committee officer Jeff Moretzsohn, from the evangelical but staid mainline Paoli congregation, the Church of the Good Samaritan said, "We will have to watch his movements for the first few months. Fr. Bangerboy has agreed to wear a criminal ankle bracelet to monitor his whereabouts, but we think that is a short-term thing. He can't possibly be as bad as Bishop Charles Bennison whom I supported."

Members of the Standing Committee all agreed that forgiveness is the issue and God is Lord of the second chances, even for pedophiles even though there is a lot of evidence that he might regress and sexually abuse a young person again.

"He has agreed not to do confirmations, teach Sunday School and his Archdeacon will do all baptisms till we get the all clear which we think will come from above when the Holy Spirit wakes up and speaks to us," said another Standing Committee member.

A progressive priest, on hearing the news, said the Standing Committee took its cue from the recent killing of a cyclist by the drunken Suffragan Bishop of Maryland. "If the diocese can forgive her and she manages to get off with a legal slap on the wrist because she is an Episcopal bishop, then we know we are on the right track, anything is possible in TEC, and we still have a lot of money left for lawsuits if Fr. Bangerboy should regress. Of course we hope (and pray) that won't happen.

"We really had to scour the country looking for someone of his talent. We consulted the lesbian Bishop of Los Angeles Mary Glasspool and the head of Integrity, the unofficial pansexual Episcopal organization and while they recommended a transgendered priest from the Diocese of Massachusetts, we felt Fr. Bangerboy brought less sexual baggage to the altar and job. He'll be a great choice, we are all convinced of that."

The diocese did say they would be updating their insurance policies just in case.

QUALIFICATIONS FOR BEING A BISHOP IN THE EPISCOPAL CHURCH

The search committee of XXXXX says that it seeks a bishop who:

Loves the Church more than the Lord of the Church and can articulate why it is important to be an Episcopalian as opposed to being an Anglican or Roman Catholic with rigidly held views.

Whether leading a meeting, preaching and celebrating the Eucharist, or meeting one-on-one with individuals, he must be an administrative leader who can count and know when a parish is no longer viable and if it is time to close the doors and take the remaining endowment before it all runs out.

A bishop must actively tend to his own interior life and is "lit up enough" (with whiskey, hence the term Whiskeypalian) for all to see and join him/her in a fifth whenever possible.

Will lead the Diocese into a shared mission, vision and direction.
We dream of a diocese that respects the diversity of God's people

regardless of gender, age, economics, ethnicity and sexual orientation, especially the last with the hope that a transgendered person will ascend a pulpit and turn the Bible completely on its head over sexuality preferences. We as a diocese can't wait to ordain a person who is LGBTQIIIXXXxxx1212, anything less will be considered homophobic.

We seek a visionary, action-oriented leader who, after getting to know the people, structures and culture of this diocese, is prepared to help articulate and activate a congregation mostly over the age of 65 into priorities for the coming years...and beyond the grave...priorities that fully embrace our Baptismal Covenant and hope to God that anyone wearing a pants or skirt (or both) will darken the red doors before they have to close forever and allow a continuing care center be built next to the church, for those Episcopalians living beyond 92.

Equip congregations of all sizes for evangelism and mission, but under no circumstances must you tell people that they are sinners in need of a savior. That is way too exclusive. We want to include everybody under the banner of the Jesus Movement and "beloved community," which is basically a knockoff of the reign of God but more secular and inclusive.

We want to embrace Presiding Bishop Michael Curry's call for evangelism, however that is defined, as part of the Jesus Movement which we hope will excite people into smiling a lot, jumping up and down in the pulpit and talking endlessly about racism, even if the diocese can't actually spot or know a racist. (If it does turn out to be 88-year old Mildred who once called a black man "Uncle Tom", she should forthwith be excommunicated from the church).

Amid uncertainty about what the church will look like in this post-Christendom age, we seek a bishop who brings an entrepreneurial spirit and encourages holy risk-taking to help equip congregations for creative evangelism and mission in the communities we serve, especially we hope he will reach out to the LGBTQIIIXXXxx1212 community with a special focus on transgender folk who insist on using parish toilets on gay pride parade days. We believe this is an act of inclusivity at its highest.

A bishop must demonstrate a collaborative leadership style but not too much, as we don't want to upset the natural order of things. Clergy and lay people, adults and children alike, gladly bring an abundance of gifts, talents, perspectives and energy to the work they do for their churches and for the diocese. The bishop will, of course, have the last say, and if any priest or lay leader starts to show signs of spiritual life, like wanting to start Bible studies, prayer meetings for the survival of the Church and express an interest in leading people to Christ, then that person should be told to go.

A bishop must build and maintain meaningful relationships with clergy, staff and diocesan leaders. The bishop will see how much relationships matter at all levels of the diocese and how connected we are to one another (despite the miles between us). The diocese seeks a humble, pastorally minded individual who will take the time to get to know people, pay attention and be present and not touch them inappropriately, nor admit to past adulterous relationships, refrain from bullying when he can't get his way, and know how to balance a check book and to encourage youth in the church if he can find any.

A bishop who will fully support the life and ministry of small congregations. Most small congregations are actively going out of business, so it is important to find someone, anyone who can support the life of a church. The church might even be willing to fund from its endowment a person who knows how to chat up lesbitransgays and be willing to spend time at Starbucks coffee shops and local bars getting to know people. He must know how to talk up inclusion and diversity but not salvation which is way too exclusive.

With most dioceses having more than half of its churches being served by part-time, non-stipendiary or supply clergy, we seek a bishop who does not see a small congregation as a problem to be solved and who recognizes that "small and mighty" churches have as much to offer as the "large and powerful" ones. We especially need a bishop who champions knowing real estate developers who can find a buyer for when the church doors close forever.

We seek a bishop who works outside conventional structures and boundaries. A bishop should know how to listen and listen and listen, and even though he has no solutions or answers, he should show significant empathy in the face of the abyss that lies before him.

We seek a bishop who courageously engages in healthy conflict resolution. We know conflict is a normal aspect of human interactions and provides opportunity for growth. However, our recent history suggests a pattern of conflict avoidance. We seek a leader who provides a non-anxious presence and who can facilitate difficult situations and conflict in healthy, creative and constructive ways. We believe this ability requires both a steady presence and a prophetic voice. When this fails, the bishop retains the authority to throw the priest out, especially if he is orthodox in faith and morals, padlock the doors, (like the bishop did in Los Angeles), and then turn it into a mission, and put in his own man/woman who will inevitably close the doors. It's important that the right person be in place to perform this function and can give appropriate Last Rites for a church.

The most important thing to remember as a bishop is, that it doesn't matter how bad you are, you will always have a fat pension to look forward to courtesy of the Church Pension Fund which has done a better job growing your money than the Episcopal Church has done making new converts. Fiat Lux.

EPISCOPAL PRESIDING BISHOP MICHAEL CURRY SEARCHES FOR ELUSIVE EPISCOPAL RACISTS

What exactly are you doing looking under the bed, dear?

I'm looking for racists, my beloved. You know I've been telling Episcopalians for years that the church is full of racists. I preach about it as part of my Jesus Movement revival campaigns to jump start the church in the 21st century and if I'm not successful, we will be out of business in a decade or so. We have got to get the Church back on track or we are lost.

So, you think talk about racism will fill churches?

It will get people thinking and that is the important thing to do.

Well, how's that working for you?

Not good I'm afraid.

If I recall, the last public racist was John Shelby Spong, in 1998, in Canterbury at the gathering of

Primates. He made racist comments about African bishops and was forced to apologize by then

PB Frank Griswold. I haven't heard of anyone since making public racist statements. You don't think you might be beating a dead horse, do you? Most Episcopalians are now in their middle sixties and probably see blacks only on TV!

Ever since my celebrity sermon for the Royals, things have not gone as planned.

By now we should have had 10,000 new Episcopalians, but it has not happened and I'm worried because churches continue to close, dioceses are in decline and we have more funerals than any other statistic.

So, what do you plan on doing about it?

Well, for starters, I am going back under the bed and continue my search for racists, which I'm sure I'll find if I keep looking hard enough.

Well, dear, when you come up for air, your black pajamas will be on top of the white sheets. Don't forget to put them on.

EPISCOPAL CHURCH ELECTS NORMAL BISHOP

History was made this week when an openly normal man was elected Bishop of Newark, NJ.

"I'm stunned," said Presiding Bishop Michael Curry. "This man represents everything the Church no longer stands for and has publicly rejected. He is white, male, heterosexual. He has a wife and two kids and says he actually believes in Jesus as Lord and Savior, has read and believes the formularies, believes scripture is authoritative and final as the church's primary source of truth.

"What is stunning is that he got through the ecclesiastical net, especially as we now have a committee set up to pre-vet all potential bishops, and someone like this is clearly unacceptable, so I need to know how he got through the net. I am horrified."

"Such people should not get anywhere near a see these days. After all, this is the diocese of former bishop, John Shelby Spong, a world class theologian, whose 12 Theses are now the hallmark doctrines of TEC. I just added the Jesus Movement to goose it up a bit."

What we are looking for is someone who is black, bisexual or transgendered, a he/she with whatever sexual organs they claim to have, someone who was trained at Episcopal Divinity School where the Bible is opened and read only during coffee breaks, said a dejected Curry.

"We want a bishop who will focus on climate change, pansexuality and the occasional paranormal sightings just in case there is something supernatural out there that we haven't spotted."

Remember, this IS the Episcopal Church, the Church of what's happenin' now, not what happened yesterday.

END

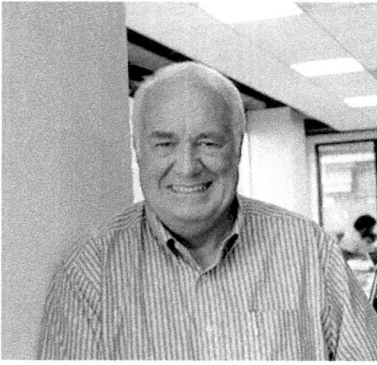

Born and raised in Wellington, New Zealand, David attended Scots College a private boys' school, in Wellington, from which he graduated in 1961. He worked for the Province newspaper as a reporter and later attended Victoria University, where he studied English and Philosophy. He went on to study for a Diploma in Theology at London Bible College. He later moved to the United States, where he undertook further theological studies at Trinity Evangelical Divinity School in Deerfield, Il, for two years, following which he completed his MCS at Regent College, University of British Columbia, Vancouver, BC.

David became Religion Editor of the Vancouver Province newspaper where he served for eight years. He moved to New York City in 1979 where he took up a position as Media Communications Director for the American Bible Society. He later accepted the position of Media Communications Director for American Leprosy Missions. He served for two years as associate pastor of an historic Black Baptist Church in Montclair, NJ. He briefly served with World Vision International as Communications Director in Ethiopia.

David became a freelance journalist and is the author of three books. His first book, A FLAME FOR JUSTICE, is on the life of Caesar Molebatsi, a visionary black pastor and leader in Soweto, South Africa. His second book, A VISION OF HOPE on the life of Samuel Habib, one of the Arab world's leading contemporary Christian leaders based in Cairo, Egypt, demonstrated a holistic approach to mission. His third book, written conjointly with the Rev. Dr. Earle Fox, on HOMOSEXUALITY: GOOD AND RIGHT IN THE EYES OF GOD? explores a contemporary culture war issue that currently bedevils the Western Church.

For the past 25 years, he has been president and lead writer for VIRTUEONLINE, the Anglican Communion's largest and most widely read orthodox Anglican Online News Service, which annually reaches over 4 million readers in 170 countries.

In 2002, he received an Honorary Doctor of Divinity from Laud Hall Theological Seminary.

David lives with his wife Mary in Philadelphia, PA. They have three grown children and three grandchildren.

www.ingramcontent.com/pod-product-compliance
Lightning Source LLC
Chambersburg PA
CBHW061432040426
42450CB00007B/1007